LA SCALA

Giorgio Lotti — Raul Radice

Introduction by Paolo Grassi
with a Reminiscence by Attilio Bertolucci

PARK LANE
New York

LA SCALA

Special thanks to Paolo Grassi, Carlo Mezzadri, Anna Prina, Erio Piccagliani, Mara Vitali Greco, Patrizia Biffi, Rosanna Locatelli

Translated from the Italian by John Gilbert

Design: Daniele Baroni

This edition is published by Park Lane, a division of Crown Publishers, Inc.

a b c d e f g h

Printed and bound in Italy by Officine Grafiche di Arnoldo Mondadori Editore, Verona
Library of Congress Cataloging in Publication Data

Lotti, Giorgio.
   La Scala.

   1. Teatro alla Scala.   I. Radice, Raul.
II. Title.
ML1733.8.M5L73   1981   782.1′0945′21   81-4935
ISBN 0-517-34453-X   AACR2

LA SCALA
BETWEEN
THE TWO WARS

Once again it started with the spoken word. The period is easily pinpointed—the early years of the present century. The meaning was not always clear, for often there were only isolated words and phrases that emerged from a confused babble of sound, especially when the family was seated around the dinner table, either at midday with the sun streaming through the windows or in the evening when the white tablecloth and cutlery gleamed in the gaslight. Every now and then the lamp would flicker and fade, and a candle had to be hastily summoned so that the mantle could be replaced—a tricky operation in the semidarkness. But how delightful it was, when shadow fell over the room, to savour the tantalizing aroma of the soup in the steaming tureen or, if you had already been served, in your plate. A sepulchral voice in the darkness might make a remark about the Witches' Sabbath and the misty gloom over the peak of the Brocken. There would be general laughter, light would eventually be restored, and the eating and conversation would resume.

On such occasions the little boy, at last privileged to join the adults for dinner, heard for the first time names of musicians and singers as well as the titles of operas that were to remain fixed in his mind. For the most part these titles were the same as those that he later discovered printed on the scores propped up on the music stand next to the piano. When he was old enough to read them he would associate them with the marvellous pictures decorating the covers—the young man in a white shirt clambering down from a high wall while the blindfolded Rigoletto obligingly held the ladder; the beautiful Violetta, a golden figure against a rosy background, holding a cup brimming over with sparkling wine; and Aïda, in the sealed tomb below the Temple of Vulcan, dying in the arms of her beloved Radames. For the first time he read the names of Verdi, Bellini, Rossini, Donizetti, and later of Mascagni, Puccini, and Wagner. Later still, he was to become familiar with Richard Strauss, Moussorgsky, Rimsky-Korsakov, Debussy, and Ravel, and then, tumbling out in a flood, such names as Wolf-Ferrari, Cilèa, Giordano, Pizzetti, Zandonai, Montemezzi, Pick-Mangiagalli, Alfano, and Respighi. In the course of his teens he would, of course, have his particular favourites and one or two pet aversions, but for the time being all were equally fascinating. Sometimes underneath the great names printed in large letters there were others, in smaller type. One, which conjured up a vision of distant, unknown lands, was that of Michele Saladino, noted for his transpositions of many famous operas

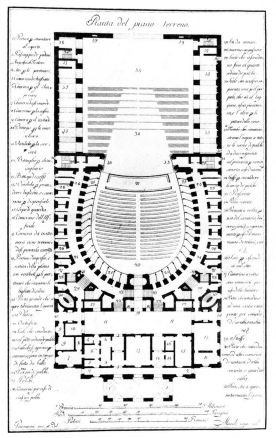

Giuseppe Piermarini's planimetry of the ground floor of the Teatro alla Scala.

for performance on the piano. His name appeared, for example, on the cover of Boito's *Mefistofele,* which was always prominent among the scores and frequently left open on the piano stand. Now and then a young aunt would work her way through a few pages of the score, sometimes with restrained vocal accompaniment (it could hardly be called singing): "Great and wise cavalier, let me know again why you love me—the village maiden with her simple country ways?" Or "Last night they hurled my baby into the depths of the sea. . . ." It was a great favourite with the family.

All these names, at one time or another, centered naturally around one place, the Teatro alla Scala (or simply La Scala, as it was familiarly called). But conversation around the dinner table also dwelt on names from more distant parts—mysterious characters involved in events that, so far as the child was aware, were totally unconnected. Only later would he associate such anecdotes with the life and history of that famous opera house. As yet the very name meant nothing to him. He did not have the faintest idea what a "theatre" might be. It was just another word.

The names cropped up in adult conversation like islands in an uncharted sea, casually mentioned in the context of an anecdote, a newspaper report, or a piece of gossip. Often he was completely mystified by them. There was talk of Armida and the wonderful fountains that graced the garden. What a pity the magical illusion had to be shattered by the massive figure of Eugenia Burzio, a singer with a tremendous voice and a body to match it—"a woman you had to listen to without looking at her." Mention was made of a recent, highly attractive acquisition, the lovely Rosina Storchio, an incomparable Norina whose charms were apparent even to the conductors of the orchestra. Her photograph stood on a sideboard in the drawing room together with that of Virginia Reiter, another paragon, by contemporary standards, of feminine allurement. Praise was given to Bonci for the marvellous way in which he mingled laughter and singing in his *Ballo in Maschera* cabaletta ("It's a joke or lunacy, this prophecy: but what is most ludicrous is how they believe it"); and regret was expressed because Enrico Caruso was now so rarely heard in Italy. They spoke enthusiastically of the Marseilles-born baritone Victor Maurel, chosen by Verdi to sing Iago in the first performance of *Otello* in 1887, notable, among other things, for the moustache incident. At that time most men wore bushy whiskers with upward-turned tips. Those gentlemen not adorned in this manner were scornfully dismissed as "Americans or priests." Maurel, a handsome fellow, was extremely proud of his moustache. Verdi, however, could not imagine his Iago thus equipped. He himself sported a fine, carefully cultivated set of whiskers for more than twenty years and was well aware of the distress he was causing Maurel in asking him to shave off his own completely. The baritone agreed. Six years later Verdi chose him as his first Falstaff.

Mention of *Falstaff* brought the conversation around to another nostalgic family event. The father was at this point persuaded to leave the table and remove from a drawer in his study a photograph which was by now slightly faded in spite of its protective transparent covering. It showed a group of about twenty young men, evidently waiting for something; and below it was scribbled a date: "9 February 1893." Beneath that, in the same handwriting, was added: "7:30 in the morning." This was how the boy came to learn that this was the date of the world premiere of Verdi's last opera. The gray wall which took up most of the photograph was the left-hand side of La Scala; and these early risers were, in fact, standing in front of the entrance to the top gallery, the door to which would not be opened before seven in the evening. The real point of interest was that the tall, thin lad towering over the rest of the group was his own father, then not yet twenty years old, who on that day had played truant from the law school that he attended in Pavia. A friend who had wandered along to see this unusual, though not wholly unpredictable, gathering had taken the photograph and given his father a copy; and with the aid of a magnifying glass and by holding the picture in a good light and at the correct distance, one could just make out the features of the people concerned.

Invariably, and especially if there were relatives or casual acquaintances present, the sight of the photograph provoked a spate of questions. What was the weather like on that February morning? Answer: As cold as it usually is in Milan at that time of year. What did they all do to while away that long wait (twelve hours without any place to sit down)? Presumably food was no problem since surely they had brought along plenty of tasty rolls; but had anyone thought of a way of getting hold of a hot drink?
With a smile the father would reply that, as far as he could recall, at the age of twenty nobody was greatly worried about standing or particularly conscious of hunger and thirst. In any case, the "importance of the event" had put everyone in a cheerful mood, and he still looked back to that famous day with pleasure and pride.

By now it was time for the little boy to go to bed. He had said his prayers, kissed his mother good night, and heard the door click shut. For a while the coldness of the sheets kept him awake. His sleepy gaze fastened on the pink lampshade standing on the chest of drawers beside his bed and the flickering flame of the small candle inside it. Now and then, from the street below, which linked the Piazza San Giovanni in Conci and the Piazza Sant'Alessandro, he heard the sound of a passing cab, the steady trot of the horses and the tinkling of their harness bells. And sometimes the silence would be broken by the tipsy laughter of revellers or, more rewardingly, by a clear, melodious, and remarkably beautiful voice singing an operatic aria, the words of which were distinct even if not comprehended: *"Spirto gentil . . . gentle spirit of light, in my dreams you shine. . . ."*

A corner of Arrigo Boito's study in Milan.

The singer, returning home, was a young man whose splendid tenor voice was familiar to everyone in the neighbourhood. Rumour had it that he was the son of a janitor at the Liceo Beccaria. His name was Giuseppe Armanini, and within some ten years he was to become a regular singer at La Scala. The child who often heard that song when just dropping off to sleep would hear it

The composer Pietro Mascagni.

again and see the actions accompanying the words when he was a grown boy; and Armanini was singing in the first two operas, never to be forgotten, that he ever attended—Humperdinck's *Die Königskinder* and Cimarosa's *Il Matrimonio Segreto.*

After words came pictures. Lying around the house were magazines, calendars, issues of *Illustrazione Italiana,* and even cards given away with packets of Liebig's meat extract, showing the facade of La Scala and, more exciting still, the inside of the auditorium with its rows of boxes and closed curtains, looking like windows concealing all manner of mysteries and intrigues.

Occasionally the boy would thumb through the pages of a book or magazine and come across a coloured engraving or reproduction of an old painting that particularly caught his attention. There was a picture by Angelo Inganni, and every time the child looked at it he saw something new. He was fascinated by the play of clouds, by the counter set up beside the entrance door (although he never found out what was being sold), and by the carriage in the foreground drawn by two differently coloured horses. On the box of the cab sat a coachman and by his side a Moorish servant boy in national dress.

In the mid-nineteenth century the piazza had not yet been built. The theatre was approached by way of a rather narrow street, not so much a thoroughfare as a meeting place. It was a place where people stopped to chat and sat out on their balconies. Opposite was the Caffè del Teatro, where the famous impresario Barbaia once entertained friends and acquaintances with a drink that he had invented—a mixture of coffee, chocolate, and cream that was named *barbagliata* in his honour. The elder family aunts pointed out that Domenico Barbaia's reputation was not based entirely on this concoction, for he had launched and patronized composers such as Rossini, Bellini, and Donizetti. The very young Rossini, though not ungrateful for Barbaia's support, had nevertheless repaid him rather shabbily by running off with the beautiful Spanish singer Isabella Colbran, Barbaia's mistress. It was a good thing he had married her—a bit late, perhaps, but still in time.

Along with the pictures, the boy picked up bits and pieces of historical information about the theatre itself and how it came to be built. The Teatro Ducale had been set on fire several times, but the blaze that broke out on the evening of 25 February 1776 had completely gutted the place. Possibly it was a case of arson. This final disaster convinced the citizens and authorities that if a new theatre were to be built, it ought to go up on another site where, if not wholly immune to fire, the chances of severe devastation would be minimized. But it was far from easy to choose an alternative place. Some suggested the "Cà di can" in San Giovanni in Conca, belonging to Bernabò Visconti. Others proposed the Scuola Cannobiane, near the Ducal Palace. The Castle area, suggested, so it was rumoured, by Maria Theresa, was judged unsuitable, on the grounds that no true citizen of Milan would willingly patronize a place that was so far off the beaten track.

The Milanese were in a hurry to build their new theatre. It was not in their nature to delay matters. The boxholders, who were virtually the owners of the theatre, were particularly anxious to get moving. Ten days after the fire, in fact, they nominated three "knightly delegates" to approach the Archduke Ferdinand and request him to arrange for the immediate rebuilding of the theatre. It only took another ten days for Ferdinand to agree, on March 10; and by the end of the month the architect Giuseppe Piermarini had drawn up plans for building the new house in the neighbourhood of the Church of Santa Maria.

Piermarini, who was then a little over forty years old, was a pupil of Vanvitelli. He had been responsible for the facades of the Palazzo Belgioioso opposite the house of Manzoni, as well as the Litta and Greppi palaces. The Villa Reale in Monza (nicknamed the Italian Schönbrunn) was his work, as was the facade of the Archbishopric and the fountain facing it—that great marble basin supported by two sirens sculpted by Chiari, long known to the locals as Theodolinda and regarded as a standard of comparison for other sculptors choosing to portray scantily clad women.

La Scala was inaugurated on 3 August 1778. Certainly, the theatre, as shown in contemporary prints, differs in some respects from the building that stands there today. On the left-hand side, as one looks at it, there was originally no Casa Ricordi, the publishing house that was later established there and which played such a prestigious role in the musical life of the city; and a few years afterward the left wing of the building was to accommodate the Museo Teatrale, which, though not envisaged by Piermarini, would become the logical complement of the opera house itself.

The engravings collected by the family, as well as the picture by Inganni, testified to the majestic appearance of the street on the right side of La Scala. A small alley dedicated to Saint Joseph had been greatly enlarged to make room for an impressive precinct, famous, among other things, for accommodating the headquarters of the Patriotic Society as well as the Cova restaurant and café, serving the local cake that was later to be known as the *"panettone delle Tre Marie, much loved by Verdi."*

After his death, the Via San Giuseppe was renamed in Verdi's honour; and the Milanese, when bringing it up in the course of casual conversation, would, as like as not, refer to it as the "Via San Giuseppe Verdi." Some of them still call it that today. And nowadays, a little way past the Hotel Milan, someone will be sure to wave an arm toward the corner window of the hotel room in which the composer died. The room's furniture has since been handed over to the Musicians' Rest Home, but it was here that Verdi spent his last six, agonizing days. Everyone knew he was dying. The authorities strewed a thick layer of straw over the road under the window so that the ailing composer should not be disturbed; and people waited outside the hotel

Cover of the libretto of Mascagni's *Cavalleria Rusticana.*

for news. On 1 February 1901 Verdi left his Milanese home on his last journey. He was carried in a pauper's hearse, followed by two priests and an enormous crowd, to the Cimitero Monumentale.

After familiarizing himself with the history and appearance of the outside of La Scala, the boy gradually picked up scraps of information about the interior of the house. He came to know the reason for those half-closed curtains in front of the boxes. They were there to ensure the privacy of the occupants who treated the opera house as their own home. Of course they went to La Scala to listen to music, but that was only a part of it. It was a place for playing games, for dining, and for receiving friends. Here new marriages were arranged and old marriages frequently broken up. They conversed, they gossiped, and they intrigued. The boy heard his elders speak, without much particular concern for sequence or dates, of Napoleon Bonaparte, the Ballo del Papa, the Congress of Vienna and the Serata dello Scappellotto, of Stendhal and Byron, or the Marquis Giorgio Pallavicino and Count Federico Confalonieri. They recalled with pride the famous Five Days of 1848, when a barricade was raised outside the opera house itself, reinforced, among other materials, by the theatre's own archives, never to be recovered ("a real shame," some said; "but not the worst of misfortunes," said others, without making it clear whether their skepticism was genuine or pretended).

What confused the lad most was the frequent reference to the "boxholders," evidently a special sect whose true significance he had not yet grasped. He came to realize, however, that it was a society composed of people with breeding and wealth, which was judged to be beneficial or harmful, according to your point of view. But nobody had much good to say of the Comune, not exactly renowned for its farsightedness, with whom the "governing body" of boxholders (another name that was to stick in his memory) talked and argued about a grant that would enable them to organize the opera season—a matter on which agreement was never reached. So 1901 was an unlucky year, remembered mainly because of the quarrels over the grant. All citizens listed on the electoral register were invited to give their opinion on the subject, and there were twice as many votes against the proposal than for it. The implication was that La Scala was the private business of the boxholders and not an essential element of the city's cultural life.

Fortunately salvation was at hand, in the guise of the Visconti family from Modrone. The Visconti dukes and counts owned half a dozen boxes among them. In spite of their noble lineage they were active in encouraging the city's industrial development, and all of them, in some measure, were lovers and supporters of the arts. For some time the Visconti family had helped to maintain the prestige of La Scala, often finding the necessary funds themselves. Back in 1833 Duke Charles had been made the theatre's manager, and in May of that year he had welcomed to La Scala María Felicía Malibran, who came to sing Rossini's *Otello* and, in rivalry with Giuditta Pasta, *Norma*. Malibran's visit to Milan was a memorable event (she died six years later in Manchester as a result of falling from a horse), and the duke had organized a farewell party in her honour in the garden of his palace in Via della Cerva. The evening included a special serenade to the singer played by the Scala orchestra.

Now, once more, another Visconti, Duke Guido, headed the delegation of boxholders. With commendable shrewdness, he had restored the theatre's reputation by entrusting the rehearsals and conducting of the Scala operas to a young musician named Arturo Toscanini. It was said of him that he was the most talented of the lot and that it was a pity that he had such a bad character. One evening, for example, he walked off the rostrum after conducting two acts of *Un Ballo in Maschera,* leaving the opera unfinished. For the first time, too, the post of artistic and administrative director went to another young man, the thirty-year-old Giulio Gatti-Casazza, by profession a marine engineer but also a music lover who arrived at La Scala after having directed the Teatro Comunale at Ferrara for five years. Ferrara, admittedly, was not Milan, but its citizens knew their music and were hard to please. Unfortunately, well-informed folk were now saying that Gatti-Casazza was also on the point of leaving La Scala. The rumour was that he was wanted by the Metropolitan in New York, another famous opera house where, as the Milanese were quick to point out, singers would perform only after having first appeared at La Scala.

La Scala, despite all controversies and its periodic ups and downs, was the institution that handed out the diplomas, described as "perhaps the greatest opera house in the world . . . of which the Milanese had good reason to be proud." The members of the family never tired of discussing the theatre, what had happened there and what was likely to happen in the future. While the season was still on, talk revolved around the operas then being staged; and as soon as it was over, there was conjecture and gossip and, sometimes, reliable information about next year's program. Discussion would begin in mid-autumn and reach fever pitch in the days immediately preceding the appearance of the bills for the new season, especially if the newspapers had mentioned the title of this or that opera and the names of particular singers and conductors.

So there was eager expectation of the opera that was to be chosen to open the new season. La Scala traditionally reopened on the evening of December 26, Saint Stephen's Day; and since this was immediately after Christmas Day, the boy came to think of it as a continuous festival, anticipating still more festive occasions such as the ball that customarily took place on the stage and in the stalls. The latter usually occurred on the last Friday of Carnival and was a central topic of conversation at the lunch and dinner table. There was much discussion about the name to be given to the ball (the next would be called "La Scala d'Oro"), the excitement generated, the fancy-dress costumes that the regulars had worn on past occasions and might be wearing this time, the elegance (and sometimes the daring) of the women, the lavishness and expense of it all. One year a group of six or seven young men—aristocrats, painters, and professionals—had staggered out of La Scala at four in the morning, gone straight to the station just as they were, in tails and white tie, and boarded the first train for Vienna. Two days later they returned from the Austrian capital, still in evening dress.

Francesco Tamagno in the first *Otello* at La Scala (1887).

"Sheer madness," of course; but quite in keeping with the theatre's history and character. Worth remembering and worth mentioning from time to time. After all, "a little tolerance never did any harm."

After the pictures, the actuality. The whole family—father, mother, and the three boys—would visit La Scala three or four times a year. The parents, unaccompanied by their sons, would also go on special occasions, perhaps invited by friends to share their box. The father would never miss a production and in the case of certain operas would not be satisfied with a single visit. He was one of the regulars of the gallery, the second of which usually cost two lire, but only one lira on popular nights and a mere fifty centesimi for "very popular" performances.

The family outing was a very special event. The boys were taken to La Scala for educational purposes, either to enrich their store of culture or to fill their minds with images that they would remember later, but seldom for pure entertainment in the accepted sense of the word. Obviously it was an expense and the money had to be set aside. For reasons of economy the family would make for the gallery, but not necessarily the second. More often, they would choose the less crowded first gallery on the floor below, not in the standing room, of course, but in the first row of numbered seats on the rail, difficult to come by at the box office but usually available, on payment of a bit extra, from one of the many touts swarming around the theatre. Everyone agreed that this traffic was amoral and illegal but nobody ever succeeded in stamping it out.

Visits to La Scala were confined to the evening before a holiday and proper dress was obligatory. It was only a short distance from home to the opera house and the family would go on foot. There was no real rush, provided one had left on time, yet there was an irrepressible urge to get a move on, because until one turned into Santa Margherita, there was always a nagging fear that La Scala might be closed that evening owing to unforeseen circumstances.

What a relief it was, then, once past the monument to Carlo Cattaneo, to see the two lamps on the terrace which dominated the portico and entrance to the main lobby. The warm light flooding the street seemed to extend a welcome, and in the later war years one was keenly conscious of its absence. After that reassuring glimpse of the opera house, the pace would slacken again for the leisurely climb up the seemingly endless flight of steps. A brief halt at the cloakroom and finally the family would take its seats, with a stern warning to the boys not to drop anything down into the stalls. Mother's handbag would be ceremoniously opened and out would come the opera libretto (from which she would recite a few lines aloud) and, better still, a handful of caramels to be shared out in turn. Father, for his part, was sole guardian of the opera glasses. Now and then he would permit the boys, one

Eugenia Burzio.

after the other, to look through them, but not for a moment would they leave his hand.

There were plenty of things to occupy the boys' attention. If they had arrived early enough they could watch the stalls gradually filling up. From the giddy heights of the gallery they would gaze down at the expensive seats below as the elegantly dressed audience trickled in, courteously ushered to their places by strangely costumed attendants. They counted the members of the orchestra (all in evening dress) as they filed into the pit, some of them holding instruments whose very names were new, such as the clownlike bassoon. They even amused themselves by trying (vainly) to count the number of lights hanging in clusters from the enormous central chandelier. An immense lamp, this, which when they first saw it prompted the tremulous inquiry as to what would happen if it accidentally fell to the ground, followed by the more practical question about the way in which all those tiny lights were replaced.

Meanwhile the confused babel of sounds from the orchestra pit would gradually rise to a climax, coinciding with the moment when the auditorium lights were dimmed and only those in the boxes remained. Then, suddenly, there was silence, the conductor entered to ringing applause, and the whole house was plunged into darkness. Up went the footlights, illuminating the red-and-gold velvet curtain which formed a barrier between present reality and a magic world of make-believe where everything was cause for surprise and wonder. The boy found it hard to tear his mind away from the marvellous events on the stage even in the intermissions, for by now the comings and goings of the people in the auditorium presented no novelty, and he was, truth to tell, a bit bored by the stream of facts churned out by his parents. He was not even particularly interested when they pointed toward the royal box—not the large box immediately above the entrance, which was used only on official ceremonial occasions, but the double box in the second tier, just to the left of the proscenium pillar. It was really two boxes in one, originally allocated in perpetuity to the Archduke Ferdinand (he had enjoyed the same privilege at the Teatro Ducale) and now, of course, belonging to the House of Savoy. The Count of Turin, who usually lived in Milan, was often to be seen sitting in it, as were various other members of the royal family.

The boy had a much clearer recollection of the single box standing on its own on the same side, but higher up at the end of the fifth tier. This was the box reserved for the Institute of the Blind in the Via Vivaio, whose inmates had used it for as long as anyone could remember. It was the only one that had been retained when the other boxes at that level were demolished to make room for the first gallery, in recognition of the fact that the blind were particularly musical. So every evening four or five blind youngsters sat motionless in that box, seeing nothing of those glittering lights but all listening with rapt attention, heads cocked to one side.

When he first went to La Scala, the boy was more interested in seeing than listening. He soon learned to identify the famous figures associated with the operas. He knew that the man on the conductor's rostrum was Tullio Serafin, then a little over thirty years old. He was conducting at La Scala for the first time but the connoisseurs were already predicting a great future for him. Singing at this performance of *Die Königskinder* was Lucrezia Bori, a very beautiful woman whose looks were only slightly marred by what her admirers called "Venus' squint"; and appearing opposite her was Giuseppe Armanini, the nocturnal street singer of those childhood years. But what engrossed him most were the things happening on the stage. The opera told the story of two children who, unknown to anyone, were actually of royal blood, he disguised as a swineherd, she being employed as a humble goosegirl. The boy would wait breathlessly for the moment when the gates of the city were flung open to announce the arrival (according to prophecy) of the new queen. And when the goosegirl appeared, bathed in sunlight, surrounded by her flock, rising in golden majesty from a sea of dazzling white, his heart missed a beat. At that magical moment even the geese fell silent. Before the opera began they could be heard babbling behind the curtain. The papers disclosed that the birds were supplied by one of the Visconti farms and that they had been given chloroform to restrict their movements and keep them quiet enough not to spoil the music. ("And what," demanded one indignant member of the audience, "is the Society for the Protection of Animals doing about that?") Later, after many adventures, the two royal children were found, exhausted and abandoned, in the heart of the forest. There they now lay dying under a huge tree, while snow began to fall gently from above, gradually covering their sleeping forms. He would dream of that snow later, it looked so real.

Similarly, when he first came to know *Lohengrin,* his overriding memory was of the swan; and in *Mosè* he was especially fascinated by the opening of the Red Sea, worked by an amazing piece of machinery devised by one of the Ansaldo family, the secrets of whose craft were passed down from generation to generation.

In due course he was to take spectacle for granted and delve more deeply into the other aspects of operatic production, so that the visual side took on secondary importance, a host of other impressions forging themselves on his memory. It happened during the *Königskinder* season when he saw *Il Matrimonio Segreto,* an opera that had not been given at La Scala for many years. But the great awakening really took place four years later (February 1916), when he heard his first performance of *The Barber of Seville,* staged in the opera's centenary year.

This was another opportunity for an entire family expedition. Mother was not too keen, for it was wartime, prices were going up and this would be an expensive outing. But Father had made up his mind and produced some powerful arguments to win her round. The first time she had seen *Barber,* together with the rest of the family, had been at least ten years ago, when Barrientos had sung the role of Rosina. Mother had mentioned it again and again over the years as a truly memorable occasion. Father now bombarded her with questions. What did she remember? What had she done earlier in the day, what food had she eaten, had it been fine or raining? Of course, Mother couldn't remember a thing. But what about the performance in the evening? There was Barrientos herself, the baritone De Luca, the tenor De Lucia, the bass Gaudio. She remembered every smallest detail, didn't she? Obviously, Father concluded triumphantly, routine everyday activities had been blotted into insignificance by that unforgettable performance. Need he say more? The opera was the important thing and this revival was not to be missed.

His argument prevailed, and now the boy, too, was able to sample for the first time the delights of Rossini's masterpiece. The singers included Elvira de Hidalgo, the tenor Perea, Riccardo Stracciari, and Antonio Pini-Corsi, while Gino Marinuzzi, another recent arrival, stood on the "famous podium." It was an incomparable experience in which everything taking place on the stage—events and characters—was wondrously transformed into music, something to be heard rather than seen. Afterward, as he came out into the street and walked home, he was unusually quiet. What emerged most clearly from a mass of impressions was that the music mattered far more than the stage spectacle.

Gabriele d'Annunzio at the beginning of the century.

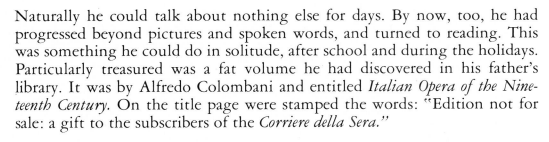

Naturally he could talk about nothing else for days. By now, too, he had progressed beyond pictures and spoken words, and turned to reading. This was something he could do in solitude, after school and during the holidays. Particularly treasured was a fat volume he had discovered in his father's library. It was by Alfredo Colombani and entitled *Italian Opera of the Nineteenth Century*. On the title page were stamped the words: "Edition not for sale: a gift to the subscribers of the *Corriere della Sera*."

The book devoted a good deal of space to La Scala but also to equally famous opera houses—the San Carlo in Naples, the Fenice in Venice, the Bologna Comunale and the Florence Pergola, the Reggio in Turin, the Piccinni at Bari, and the Bellini in Catania. And he came to learn the names of musicians who were seldom mentioned in conversation, such as Sacchini, Guglielmi, Salieri, Spontini, Cherubini, Federici, Farinelli, Simone Mayr, and Ferdinando Paër. But of course the book was mainly concerned with Rossini, Bellini, Donizetti, and Verdi, the four great composers whose statues stood in the Scala entrance hall, and were here reproduced in photographs. Richly illustrated, Colombani's book contained brief but informative biographies of the composers, descriptions of their works, fascinating anecdotes, and informal pictures.

Rossini, for example, had packed an astonishing amount of creative activity into his comparatively short career. A detailed engraving showed the impressive tribute paid him at his funeral in Paris, and alongside this was a letter in his own handwriting which threw a revealing light on his character. It was written to Giuseppe Bellentani from Modena and was dated 3 December 1853, beginning with the words: "From the so-called Swan of Pesaro to the Eagle of Estensian Sausage Men: You have wanted to impress me by soaring very high, by bestowing upon me specially prepared *zamponi* and *cappelletti*. . . ."

After hearing *Il Pirata,* Rossini had said to Vincenzo Bellini: "I am satisfied with your music. How fortunate you are to be beginning when the others are finishing." The plots of Bellini's operas—*La Straniera, La Sonnambula, I Puritani,* and *Norma*—were, of course, outlined; and associated with these were names of people and places, some of which were already familiar, such as the "Lombard Juno" Giuditta Turina, the librettist Felice Romani, and the Villa Passalacqua, at Moltrasio where Bellini had written *La Sonnambula.* There, too, were the lines written in verse on the plaque commemorating the composition of *La Straniera* at the Villa Antona Traversi at Desio: "Here among the restive whispering of the wind, when evening falls, the sad lament of a woman is heard. . . ."

Of the four composers, it was Donizetti who perhaps had the closest links with La Scala, for of the sixty-one operas he wrote, thirty-four were performed there and six written especially for it. But he always came back to his native Bergamo, to the Palazzo Scotti, where he eventually died, to the Church of Santa Maria Maggiore, where Velz commemorated him with a monument, and to the Osteria dei Tre Gobbi, here reproduced in a picture that showed the composer with his friends Mayr, Dolci, Bettinelli, and the painter Deleidi, nicknamed "Il Nebbia." This painting was, in fact, by Deleidi himself.

In 1900, when Colombani's book was published, Verdi was still alive, and the author's attitude toward him was one of reverence. The pictures associated with him went back to the early days (the farm at Roncole, his first friends Antonio Barezzi, Margherita Barezzi, Ferdinando Provesi, a radiant Giuseppina Strepponi, Temistocle Solera, Francesco Maria Piave, and Antonio Ghislanzoni) and ended up with others that had by now become famous. These showed Verdi with Boito in the Villa di Sant'Agata, the sitting room of his apartment in the Hotel Milan; the composer seated at a table together with Stoltz, his first Aïda, and other friends who met regularly every year to take the waters at Montecatini; beside Francesco Tamagno (that unforgettable Otello); alone in a wicker armchair; and standing with an umbrella suitable for protection both against rain and sun. Below the last photographs was written *"Vecchiaia verde."*

More eloquent and revealing than standard biographical notes was a kind of anthology, consisting of entire pages in parentheses, from the pens of other contemporary writers, ranging from Antonio Giulio Barrili to Giuseppe Giacosa. Such passages were neither over-effusive nor evasive, and between the lines one could get an idea of the difficult relationship that existed between Verdi and La Scala. Any opera house that had dealings with Verdi could expect trouble, but his collaboration with La Scala was particularly stormy.

Could it be, however, that tempestuous events such as these were part and parcel of musical life in general, provoked by the uncertain temperaments of those professionally involved? One of Colombani's later chapters, entitled "The Young," seemed to bear this out. It dealt with Franchetti, Pietro Mascagni ("sentenced to one masterpiece"), Puccini, Leoncavallo, and Umberto Giordano, names that were on everyone's lips, both in and out of the home. Mascagni, for example, would be well advised to give up some of his eccentricities (such as wearing unmatched red and white socks). *Madama Butterfly,* on its first night at La Scala, had been roundly jeered, but that was nothing compared with its reception nowadays (the second and third acts were played without interruption, giving some idea of the length of time that Cio-Cio-San waited for Pinkerton's return; it would have seemed even longer if that interminable act had actually gone on all night). As for Giordano, he had not only stayed at the Hotel Milan—like Verdi—but had also married one of the owner's daughters, Signorina Spatz. (And Mascagni, once again, not finding his shoes in the corridor and having shouted unsuccessfully for the chambermaid, had rushed to the top of the stairs and yelled: "My shoes, my shoes! What the devil is that Giordano up to?") Leoncavallo, everyone agreed, was after all not as good as the others. And so one piece of gossip followed hot on the heels of another, ending, as often as not, with the almost obligatory chorus that although Puccini showed great shrewdness in choosing his libretti, the same could not be said of Mascagni.

Victor Maurel in *Falstaff* (1893).

In this chapter about the younger composers there was an excellent photograph of Franchetti and Puccini seated at a spinet, and Mascagni standing beside them, showing them both a sheet of music. The same photograph was featured in a caricature by Cagnoni which appeared in the humorous newspaper *Guerin Meschino,* with the following lines printed underneath: *"Hin i speranz d'Italia in del sonà / s'hin miss d'accord per fass fotografà / ma, in fatto, tra de lor van poeu d'accord / come Sonzogn col T. del G. Ricord!"*

The meaning of this quatrain in dialect would be lost on anyone not familiar with the activities of the music copying and publishing house founded by the violinist Giovanni Ricordi and that begun by Edoardo Sonzogno, which in time came to be grim rivals for the privilege of publishing the works of the new Italian composers as well as operatic composers from abroad. This competition, apart from relatively minor disputes and jealousies (Mascagni, on Sonzogno's list, gave *Iris* to Ricordi, while Puccini, one of Ricordi's clients, took *La Rondine* to Sonzogno), was by and large a good thing for Milan and its musical life. It led Sonzogno, for example, to acquire the old Teatro della Cannobiana, to rename it the Teatro Lirico Internazionale, and to use it for staging important new operas in competition with La Scala.

The more knowledgeable citizens of Milan saw this as yet another sign of the supremacy of La Scala, which in addition to its own creative activity helped to stimulate that of other opera houses. After all, something very similar had happened before in the case of the justly famed 1830–31 season at the Teatro Carcano. Furthermore, the Teatro dal Verme, which put on a season of operas

Arturo Toscanini.

Angelica Catalani.

every autumn, while not in any sense attempting to rival La Scala, could well be regarded as an excellent training ground for aspiring musicians and singers.

Most people, therefore, saw Ricordi and Sonzogno not as rivals but as collaborators; and it was appropriate that both houses should display their wares on opposite sides of the Galleria, Ricordi's shop being in the Via Berchet and Sonzogno's in the Via Tommaso Grossi. In their splendid windows were beautifully arranged and expensive editions of operas old and modern; and through the windows one could see inside where there were portraits of composers and performers as well as wall posters portraying some of the great scenes from the operas with which the respective publishing houses had been associated. Here were coloured portraits of Verdi and Boito, together with posters that had adorned the walls of the city in former years—another chance to see Christopher Columbus sighting the New World from the helm of his ship, or the body of Scarpia laid out on the floor with Floria Tosca placing candles beside it. The poster for *Iris* was perhaps a little too symbolic; a newer one for *Isabeau,* far more exciting, showed a naked lady, covered only by her long tresses of hair, riding a horse. On one poster, displaying *L'Amore dei Tre Re,* the name of Italo Montemezzi appeared for the first time.

The boy would stop to look at these pictures whenever he happened to be passing by. If he was not too late he pressed on to another music shop near the Conservatory. Sometimes he would wander in the direction of the Villa Milius and walk down the street where Arrigo Boito lived. When someone had pointed it out to him he had been a bit afraid, perhaps uneasy at the thought of a composer who preferred working in the dark. From there he would go on to another, even quieter street. Here, for a short time, lived Alfredo Catalani, in a house which now bore a plaque. The boy never tired of looking at the slab of marble from Candoglia (the same as was used for the Duomo), on which he read these words: "Edmea, Dejanice, Loreley, and Wally have departed this life. The harp hangs from the willow, but its strings still vibrate, plucked by fingers that our eyes can no longer see." Moving words, written by Giovanni Pascoli.

As the years passed, memories crowded fast upon one another. He heard a new opera, *Francesca da Rimini,* by Riccardo Zandonai. The leading role was sung by Rosa Raïsa and with her in the cast were two newcomers, Aureliano Pertile, singing Paolo, and the very young Toti dal Monte. She made her mark with the audience not only because of her voice but also by reason of the fact that in the final act, at the moment when Francesca died, her hand really could not reach the flaming torch: "O Biancofiore, how small you are! I cannot reach your little lamp. You are the softest, smallest dove!" He remembered Massenet's *Manon* on the night when Bonci was replaced by a new young tenor, soon to reach the top, Tito Schipa. A year later there was

Mignon, with Rosina Storchio (so often talked about at home) as the heroine, and Angelo Scandiani, who was to return in different guise to La Scala some years later, as Lotario. And in the following year, on a memorable night, 3 November 1918, he saw Montemezzi's *La Nave.*

The boy was by now grown up and was allowed to go out on his own. He had come to realize that La Scala was not merely an opera house but also, as one devoted writer put it, "a solemn temple for political demonstrations by all social ranks." There were events such as the Exhibition of 1906, the Messina earthquake of 1908, and the exodus of the Friuli refugees, when no opera performances were held. But *La Nave* was surely different, associated as it was with Aquileia and the "most bitter" Adriatic, so frequently mentioned during three years of war. No opera, one would have thought, could have been more apt—even if the choice was simply coincidental—to arouse the passions of an audience which had just received the news that the war had been brought to a victorious conclusion. But quite the contrary. The regular boxholders applauded Maestro Serafin when he made a short speech before raising his baton; but most of the audience seemed to show no emotion whatsoever. Were they too deeply moved? Could they not believe the news? Were they frightened? A couple of weeks later, the atmosphere was not noticeably warmer for the commemorative evening in honour of Arrigo Boito, who had died some months earlier.

The boy was now a regular "gallery-goer," although he did not yet feel that he belonged to that privileged group which maintained, and doubtless believed, that the splendid acoustics of La Scala were incomparably finer here up in the heights. He was, however, sensitive to the atmosphere of the place and not the only one to feel that with the world greatly changed by the war things were not quite the same at La Scala as before. Some of the more enlightened boxholders clearly felt that it would be better if they gave up some of their hereditary rights, and were even prepared to do so without waiting to be asked. But of course others held different views, maintaining that "the boxholders' delegation had sometimes been guilty of mistakes but nevertheless had its good points." Most important, nobody could accuse it of having kept La Scala back. There were many things to be said in its favour. For example, it had staged *Parsifal* (shortly after the expiry of the period when performances were confined to Bayreuth) even in the fateful year of 1914. It had run for twenty-seven nights—a record achieved by no other opera in the repertoire.

During that period all sorts of names and subjects cropped up in conversation, both among the boxholders and in the Comune. There was talk of the Italian Orchestral Union, the Famiglia Artistica, the Chamber of Commerce and the Cooperative Society, the mayors Gabba and Caldara, the lawyer Majno, the Ricordi and Sonzogno publishing houses, and the theatre critics, headed by the veteran Giambattista Nappi. Nappi, who had made his reputation with *Perseveranza,* was a man of great frankness and honesty, who had a particular soft spot for Alberto Franchetti, maintaining that Verdi, after hearing *Cristoforo Colombo* at Genoa, had said of its author: "He is a real musician."

When he told this story, as he did very often, Nappi would stroke his gray beard and add insistently: "Do you know how important that is?"

Topics of broader scope were discussed all over the city, in society circles and in the streets. There was particular excitement over the news that great progress was being made toward transforming La Scala into a self-governing corporation and that supporters of the scheme included Mayor Caldara ("an enlightened Socialist"), Arturo Toscanini, who had promised the corporation his support for at least three years, and Senator Luigi Albertini, who threw in the weight and authority of the *Corriere della Sera* behind the plan.

There was talk, too, of benefactors, of a supplementary tax for subsidizing La Scala (strongly opposed, naturally, by those who had to pay it—cinemas, theatres, racecourses, football stadiums and the like), of the pros and cons of an initial nine-year experimental contract, and finally of the need to renovate the stage and provide it with more up-to-date equipment. This operation, were it to be carried out, would mean that the house would have to be closed for at least two years.

Every new piece of news and every rumour generated fresh arguments and questions. Was the building sufficiently strong to accommodate the proposed improvements without endangering Piermarini's original structure? Was it really essential to make room for new cafés, shops, and the like around the opera house? Would it not be a risky procedure, in order to enlarge the stage, to reduce the supporting roof pillars from twelve to six? And was it absolutely necessary, as a means of building a movable platform for the orchestra, to do away with the proscenium, that part of the stage that jutted out into the auditorium, which, apart from anything else, "allowed the singers to feel that they were actually in the stalls—an advantage both to themselves and to the audience"?

Eventually it was confirmed that the self-governing corporation was about to assume legal status and that an agreement had been signed between the Comune and the boxholders for a probable period of nine years. This was followed by news that Toscanini had been appointed as general artistic director and the engineer Angelo Scandiani as director-general. Like Gatti-Casazza, also an engineer, Scandiani was a lover and connoisseur of music, but was also familiar with city problems (a few years after gaining his degree he had many times covered the main streets of Milan on foot in order to draw up plans for the city's first tramway system). The new administrator stated publicly that "there was no incompatibility between pragmatism and the arts." In his exploratory work for the urban tramway, he had been accompanied by a colleague named Marco Castoldi, another music lover, who owned a business specializing in patents and who was music critic for *L'Italia,* the daily Catholic newspaper in Lombardy. The Milanese certainly knew how to get things done.

So La Scala, which had closed its doors at the end of 1918, planned a reopening about three years later. Only once was the entrance door to the stalls flung open during that time, and few were there on the day when the "Fortuny dome" was carried into the building. This was a huge, umbrellalike contraption, measuring 21 meters across, which, when open, was designed to provide the stage with a permanent ceiling. (It was used for a while "but only as an experiment.") To get it in, all traffic in the piazza had to be stopped. Meanwhile opera buffs waited patiently, some of them transferring their allegiance temporarily to other opera houses such as the Lirico, the Dal Verme, and even the Carcano. Those regular patrons of La Scala, now obliged to change their musical habits, were in for some surprises. Diaghilev's Ballets Russes, for example, was very different from the fare to which they had been accustomed—ballets such as *Excelsior,* periodically updated (the most recent performance had included telegraph boys and an airship as a tribute to Zeppelin and Forlanini), *Sieba,* and, for those with a taste for history, *Pietro Micca.* So different, in fact, that it was poorly attended. The pundits said that even if Diaghilev had appeared at La Scala (and it was just as well that it was closed) the company would not have had a better reception.

Puccini's study at Torre del Lago.

Poster for Puccini's *Madama Butterfly.*

Meanwhile, Toscanini had been busy assembling a body of musicians who would later form the orchestra of the new corporation. For the time being they gained experience by giving concert tours, planning to visit the United States and Canada, among other places. It was common knowledge that the maestro was throwing himself into the job of forming his new orchestra with extraordinary dedication. Each instrumentalist, so it was rumoured, was chosen individually; and if he heard of a musician who had once shown talent and who, because of adverse circumstances or misfortune, had dropped out of the public eye, he would personally call on him at home with a view to enlisting his services.

When the orchestra was complete it gave a memorable series of concerts in the great hall of the Conservatory, giving audiences a foretaste of musical pleasures to come when the new Scala reopened. The boy was again in the gallery (by far the best place to see Toscanini in action, despite the fact that the hall's acoustics were not all that wonderful) and was captivated by the wide range of music contained in the programs. Suddenly he realized how much new music there was to discover (as, for example, Stravinsky's *Petrushka*) and how music that he thought he knew sounded altogether different in the hands of Toscanini, who conducted the Prelude and *Liebestod* from *Tristan und Isolde,* or Victor de Sabata, appointed by Toscanini, conducting the Prelude from Act III of *La Traviata* at the end of the season.

Finally, after what seemed an interminable wait, La Scala reopened on the night of 26 December 1921. The opera chosen was Verdi's *Falstaff,* conducted by Toscanini, with Mariano Stabile in the title role. The second production of the new season was *Parsifal,* conducted by Ettore Panizza; and that was

Theatre playbill for the premiere of *Francesca da Rimini* (1929).

followed by *Rigoletto.* It was a truly golden age of singing, with Toti dal Monte, Carlo Galeffi, and Giacomo Lauri-Volpi, later joined by Aureliano Pertile, Ezio Pinza, Gilda Dalla Rizza, Rosetta Pampanini, Luisa Bertana, Gina Cigna, Mafalda Favero, and, on special occasions, Beniamino Gigli—all of them chosen by Toscanini. Indeed, Toscanini was not only fortunate enough to be surrounded by singers with extraordinary voices but also with voices that were especially suited to or perhaps destined for individual operas. When would one ever hear again (so we gallery-goers agreed) a *Lucia di Lammermoor* of such romantic intensity as that conducted by Toscanini, with Toti dal Monte, Pertile, Pinza, and Stracciari?

Season followed season and in addition to the tested favourites, there were continual surprises and revelations—*Boris Godunov,* Charpentier's *Louise,* Pizzetti's *Debora e Jaele, The Magic Flute,* and *Pelléas et Mélisande.* Unexpected subtleties were discovered in Ermanno Wolf-Ferrari's *I Quattro Rusteghi.* There was eager anticipation to see Richard Strauss conduct his *Salome,* sung by Giulia Tess. *Tristan,* with décor by Adolphe Appia, baffled the audience; and the gallery buzzed with argument over Boito's *Nerone* and, two years later, Puccini's *Turandot,* both eagerly awaited, for different reasons. By now the youth had graduated from the second gallery to the stalls, and from time to time even found a seat in the boxes. And as his visits became more frequent and regular, especially after he acquired a daily pass, he gradually got the feeling—it was almost a physical sensation—of being part-possessor of the theatre that had once, mythlike, dominated his childhood thoughts and dreams. He came to know every corner of the house, and not only the parts reserved for the audience (stalls, foyers, boxes, and corridors), but also the sections of the theatre normally out of bounds to ordinary people.

At one concert he went up onto the stage itself—the first time that it had ever been used to seat additional members of the public. He had been promised that this seat would not only be ideal for listening but would afford the extra fascination of letting him watch the conductor's gestures and facial expressions, an experience which might give him fresh insight into the score. And so it proved. There was also the added interest of watching the rest of the audience from the performers' viewpoint, enjoying a totally unprecedented sight of the stalls, boxes, and galleries of the house, packed on this occasion with almost three thousand people.

Yet even this novelty left him with a slight sense of dissatisfaction. Here was the stage, encompassed by walls of painted canvas designed to simulate a large Imperial-style reception room; and he had the sudden urge to see, to find out all that normally went on outside the bounds of those walls. He got the strong impression that "out there" in that dark space something was stirring, even in those silent hours when everything seemed deserted. Was that the theatre's secret? Or was it symptomatic of something deeper and more mysterious—a touch of madness, perhaps?

That was what he asked himself the first time he had gone into the house, not by the main door but through the entrance approached from the Via dei

Filodrammatici, then across a dark courtyard and up a short flight of narrow steps.

After a time, once the initial curiosity had waned, the sense of uneasiness that he felt seemed not unassociated with guilt. He realized that he was enjoying a possibly undeserved privilege, but, above all, he came to be aware of how indispensable the public was to the performance, giving it completeness. A performance without an audience would make no sense. Only a lunatic such as Ludwig II of Bavaria could enjoy it.

This led to a further train of thought. On the nights of special performances he would watch the audience filing in, men and women decked out in all their finery. Most of the men would be wearing a carnation in their buttonhole, handed to them by an old woman dressed in black, including a matching boa flung loosely round her neck. Her dark hair and eyes were in keeping with her somber garb. This elderly flower woman courteously handing out posies from her large basket would never accept payment on each individual visit. All that was necessary was to give her a present at the end of the season. On these glittering occasions he found himself wondering more and more often: Which public? The new tenants of the boxes, the season-ticket holders, were for the most part elderly people. The rich industrialists and celebrated professional men who rubbed shoulders in the foyer with Pick-Mangiagalli, Umberto Giordano, Italo Montemezzi, Franco Alfano, and Vincenzo Tommasini were by and large people who cared little either for music or opera. It could be that repeated attendance might improve their taste but most of them (especially the wives) regarded a visit to La Scala as a social obligation, a place to show off their wealth. Not to do so would jeopardize their professional prestige and status in society. The men looked on the Scala foyer as an ideal place for initiating or concluding business deals.

An audience which included so few young people among its season-ticket holders—and this was evident at a glance—and which was drawn to La Scala for all the wrong reasons obviously contained too many musical illiterates and philistines. They were the sort of people who let out a sigh of relief after the first act of *Parsifal,* murmuring that even where beauty was concerned, "there was a limit beyond which one shouldn't go," and that even in Germany the audience was allowed to eat dinner between acts. After the second act of *Tristan,* someone would wryly remark that "We Latins at least get a move on when we make love." They would agree that for some time now, since Giovacchino Forzano had been appointed stage director, opera had been going forward "on the road of rejuvenation," the members of the chorus no longer being ranged in one or two straight lines, singing to the accompaniment of identical gestures, all eyes turned toward the same spot, awaiting the conductor's cue. And whenever a new opera failed to win the audience's favour, many people, and not only the philistines, would raise a matter of principle. Everyone to his own taste, but really La Scala was not a place for experiments. That didn't mean, of course, that it ought to be turned into a kind of museum, although "museums are necessary and fulfil a proper function."

The composer Italo Montemezzi.

In any case, they would argue, "museum" was hardly a justifiable term for a theatre which staged ballet with "great dignity," stimulated by genuine composers such as Pick-Mangiagalli, whose *Il Carillon Magico,* described as a "feast for the eye and ear," had already been conducted by Serafin in 1918, and whose *Mahit* was staged five years later under the baton of Antonio Guarnieri. These ballets, associated with the name of Cia Fornaroli, ballerina and choreographer, were never entrusted, as had usually been the case before, to second-rate conductors. Panizza, for example, had conducted Alfredo Casella's *Il Convento Veneziano.* Then there had been *Petrushka* and *Firebird,* both conducted by Stravinsky himself—the Scala audience's introduction to the names of Massine, Fokine, and Petipa. Vittadini's *Vecchia Milano* and Pick-Mangiagalli's *Casanova a Venezia* had given way to *The Legend of Joseph* by Richard Strauss and Hugo von Hofmannsthal. Furthermore, there were productions announced of Ravel's *La Valse* with Ida Rubinstein ("the one with the long legs") and *Bolero* ("too repetitive"), choreographed by Nijinska, sister of the great dancer launched, protected, and thwarted by Diaghilev. Both of these ballets were to be conducted by Ansermet. Of course the days of Fanny Elssler, Cerrito, and Taglioni were gone forever. But who could say what impact they would have had on modern audiences? As for opera itself, might it not already have reached a dead end? Certainly nobody would dare predict whether it might branch out in new directions or whether it was time for the funeral rites.

Idle though such speculations might be, they did nevertheless relate to practical issues. One of the young man's contemporaries, either less impressionable than he or simply in the mood for a joke, once purchased some postcards which were on sale in the foyer of the opera house together with special stamps showing scenes from various Scala operas, sending warm greetings to his friends, doubtless with tongue in cheek, from "this temple of the arts." And whenever he read reviews in the papers of premieres of Scala productions in other parts of Europe, he would be infuriated at the amount of space they devoted to the costumes of this or that singer and the stupid gossip about what they had said or even what they had been eating. He could not help smiling at the story, real or invented, concerning two young musicians, Sergio Failoni and Felice Lattuada, who, after a performance at the Dal Verme of *The Tempest,* based on Shakespeare's play and with music by Lattuada, had sent a telegram, either as a joke or out of spite, to Toscanini, signing it: "The geniuses whose sun is rising to the genius whose sun in setting." Lattuada, self-taught, had once innocently remarked to Raffaele Calzini after a performance of the Pastoral Symphony that "Beethoven is great but I can beat him for storms." Nevertheless, La Scala was now about to stage Lattuada's *Le Preziose Ridicole.* But nobody involved with the arts could expect only kindness. After all, Toscanini himself, visiting friends, had once coolly compared Brahms to a pig "which is good through and through, with nothing to throw away."

In spite of all this, nothing could shake his conviction that he was lucky to be alive during a golden age that was unlikely to be repeated. Nobody could predict how long it might last but finish it would, probably without warning or without anyone being aware that it was over. At moments when this presentiment was strong, he recalled what Igor Stravinsky had said to Guido Agosti after listening to the latter's transcription for piano of *Firebird*. "Very good. Excellent," the composer had commented as he thumbed through the pages of the score. Then he had added: "Just remove those accelerandos and rallentandos, which are superfluous. The music doesn't need to make use of motoring terms."

Giuseppe Borgatti in *Siegfried*.

That golden age did, in fact, come to an end in 1929, when the nine-year experiment of the self-governing corporation expired. The time was approaching for Toscanini's dramatic decision to leave Italy and, as it transpired, live abroad for many years. He had already accepted the post of permanent conductor of the New York Philharmonic Symphony Orchestra, and had given two enthusiastically received concerts with this orchestra at La Scala. But even before that, in spite of many successes, something had been going wrong. Probably there is no major opera house anywhere which does not run into this sort of trouble at one time or another, the causes rarely being recognized by those most closely involved. As in all forms of artistic endeavour, success and prominence, even when recognized and acclaimed, engender an awareness, at some stage, of responsibility and limitation. Perhaps La Scala was undermined by its very excellence.

Paradoxically, the policy in those years was to find substitutes for established singers before they became irreplaceable; all of which simply proved how difficult they were to replace. In any event, despite these and similar actions which provoked dismay and anger in some quarters and aroused mere curiosity or indifference in others, no crystal ball was needed to foresee the new forces that would soon be unleashed, which were to dominate the theatre's activities until the end of World War Two. In the following decade new names crowded in on one another, came and went, on the conductor's rostrum, on the stage, and behind the scenes in administration. There was heated argument in the papers, cafés, and other meeting places when a Milanese industrialist and "nonmusician," Senator Borletti, was appointed director; and when Anita Colombo, formerly secretary to the corporation, succeeded Scandiani after his sudden death, the debate reached boiling point. A woman doing that job? Also, weren't there too many conductors, and how could they all be ranked equally? Nobody disputed that Ettore Panizza, Tullio Serafin, Antonio Guarnieri, Gino Marinuzzi, and Vittorio Gui deserved to be entrusted with the more important operas. There was a warm welcome, too, for a new star—Victor de Sabata, who ascended the rostrum of La Scala for the first time on 10 April 1930, conducting *The Damnation of Faust*. But what about the others? In all honesty, who was likely to remember, a few years hence, Ferruccio Calusio, Antonicelli, Sabino, Mazzolo, Negrelli, Berrettoni, and Polzinetti?

As for the principle of woman administrators, it was true that Emma Carelli had for many years run the Costanzi in Rome. No use pointing out that times

Claude Debussy.

were different and that Carelli had recently died. Dates did not alter the facts. But as far as conductors were concerned, that was a different matter. Surely, only La Scala could have fostered the hidden, incomparably refined talent of a De Sabata.

"Outsiders" such as these, critical or actively hostile, who lumped together La Scala, the Madonnina, the *Corriere,* the Banca Commerciale, rice with saffron and *panettone,* did not regard this as the right moment to revive these well-worn topics. Now we would see, said they, whether it was La Scala that made the men or the reverse. Would the new group of directors, mindful of the fact that Rossini, Bellini, Donizetti, and Verdi (whose busts graced the entrance hall of the theatre) all came to La Scala before they were thirty, commission new composers, or would they play safe and follow the old tradition of putting on only operas that the public loved and knew by heart? And, they added, we would see whether their organizational and administrative qualities were matched by considerations of matters of taste, so often sacrificed in the interests of musical style. It was suggested, for example, that the time was ripe for doing away with the bad habit of entrusting the sets of a single production to different designers. Toscanini had conducted a *Magic Flute* in which no less than four designers—Marchioro, Rota, Rovescalli, and Santoni—had collaborated, and a *Pelléas et Mélisande* with sets by Magnoni, Marchioro, Rovescalli, and Santoni! There were other similar cases in point: two scene designers for *Butterfly,* three for *Götterdämmerung,* two for *Andrea Chénier,* three for *Siegfried,* four for *La Gioconda,* and three (surely too many) for *La Bohème.* How could any designer do his job properly under such conditions?

Perhaps it was time, too, to rely more on painters, to become less obsessed with naturalism. Who could fail to notice the contrast between the painted background forests and the "real" tree trunks on which the tenor and soprano were required to sit? What about the horses and riders loaned by the Savoy Cavalry for Boito's *Nerone,* galloping onto the stage, drawing a chariot with such gusto as to arouse fears that they would all tumble into the orchestra? In another *Nerone,* by Mascagni, apart from the horrible, spick-and-span Rome ("The most beautiful examples of the spirit of ancient Rome, as is well known, are its ruins"), there were those sheep wandering across the stage at one point. And in the *Quattro Rusteghi,* the bird's-eye view of Venice, with the Grand Canal and the Basin of St. Mark, was so faithfully reproduced that when the curtain rose the audience burst into applause just as they did for a singer or, worse, a mimic. The Milanese were so conditioned to this idea of reality that it even cropped up in conversation while they were on holiday. The previous summer, the young man had fallen in with a group of tourists at Passo di Carezza. Every evening they would sit on the hotel terrace, gazing up at the Lathemar massif in the Dolomites, an ideal spot for watching the changing colours of the sky at sunset; and on one occasion the silence was broken by a voice declaring, in rapt tones, that the scene reminded him of Valhalla, and "one might really be at La Scala."

At one time such conversations would have irritated or somehow disturbed him, but now he could look at things more dispassionately. It was no longer a time of great excitements and enthusiasms. The more new operas that were staged, the more the titles and plots seemed to merge into a single amorphous, anonymous work that lacked all individuality. This, too, had happened before at La Scala, as a glance at the long list of operas would surely testify.

Yet even now there were particular nights when he came away feeling enriched and fulfilled. Sometimes he was deeply moved by the entire opera (he never forgot the first *Tristan* conducted by De Sabata or *Don Giovanni* under Bruno Walter), sometimes only by isolated fragments, visual and musical moments that he knew would remain green in his memory, to be imprinted on his mind like a beautiful piece of poetry. Among such experiences were Siegfried Wagner (bearing an astonishing likeness to his father) conducting the *Ring* cycle; Chaliapin, majestically impressive in an unexpected revival of *Boris Godunov* (when the Marquis Ridolfi, greatly moved by the nightmare scene, pointed out the significance of the armchair in which Chaliapin "sat himself above all of us"); and the leisurely awakening of the city of Rome in the Prelude to the final act of *Tosca,* so magnificently interpreted by De Sabata. And there was another recollection of De Sabata, this time in Verdi's *Requiem* – the head so proudly erect, the body almost motionless, the forehead furrowed by two deep veins and, at a particularly dramatic and tense moment, two swelling rivulets of perspiration running down his cheeks. Finally, there was the gentle, gloomy Ermanno Wolf-Ferrari, who at the dress rehearsal of *Il Campiello* asked for more light, not only on the stage (and there wasn't much) but also in the auditorium. The aging composer still dreamed of bright, sparkling operas and saw no reason why the audience could only listen in pitch darkness, everyone blackly isolated from his neighbour. To the end of his days, Wolf-Ferrari continued to yearn for a festival of opera, which nobody, at that time, knew how to enjoy.

Tito Schipa in Cimarosa's *Il Matrimonio Segreto* (1935).

The fifteenth of August 1943. After the air raid of the previous night most of the people who had stayed in Milan and who had come through unharmed had their own cares and worries. Few could yet think clearly or had yet had time to sort out the host of impressions crowding in on their consciousness. Their immediate concern was to make sure that relatives, friends, and work colleagues were safe and sound, which meant that they had to make long journeys on foot through the devastated city. Only then did they comprehend the scope of the disaster. A thick cloud of smoke, like a permanent belt of fog, hung over the ruins. He had come back from places where battles had been fought and were still raging; and his first glimpse of the bombed heart of the city evoked conflicting sensations, some of them depressing but others surprisingly uplifting, in a way that he had never before experienced. He was interested to learn subsequently that many of his fellow citizens had reacted in very much the same manner.

Nobody could feel happy or joyful, but those he spoke to confessed to a sense of gratitude for having been spared in the midst of so much desolation.

Giacomo Lauri Volpi in *Otello*.

Obviously it was absurd even to hazard a guess at the extent of the physical damage, let alone the cultural and spiritual cost. The destruction of a historic monument was certainly not more important than the destruction of the house in which one had been born, grown up, and lived. The loss of a precious possession, treasured for years and protected from any possible mishap, was of course saddening; yet in a curious way it gave people a sense of complete freedom and renewed pleasure. But as they made an inventory of what was lost and what remained, there was the overriding concern, sometimes voiced but more often unspoken, as to what might happen next time, possibly within only a few hours, and how many more raids would occur before the war ended.

Everyone knew that La Scala had been badly hit. Bombs falling on the left-hand side of the building had ripped a gash in the roof and damaged part of the auditorium below. Flying fragments had smashed or torn holes in some of the boxes of all four tiers. The stalls and part of the stage were also hit, and further damage had been caused by water from hoses—insufficient, as it proved—brought into action to put out the fires that had broken out in various parts of the house.

In the midst of all the distress over what had happened and worries as to what might still be in store, it was not easy to discover what the majority of Milanese felt when they got the news that their opera house had been struck by bombs. Many people, undoubtedly, felt that after all, sad as it was, things could have been worse. The damage, if it stopped there, could be repaired. Others maintained that the city could do without an opera house, no matter how famous, and that when the time came for reconstruction priority would have to be given to the most necessary buildings. Such people were indignantly contradicted by others who reminded their fellow citizens that they had always had an opera house. It might be premature to talk about it at present, but whenever the theatre had, for one reason or another, been destroyed in the past, it had been rebuilt—without delay.

The wits, of course, had a field day. Some said that the harsh lottery of war had decided the fate of La Scala and solved all its problems at a single stroke, so that there was nothing left to discuss. Others approved, pointing out, half seriously and half jokingly, that the city center was getting more and more constricted every day and that now the Piazza della Scala could be enlarged so as to include the area once occupied by the opera house, and used for building an enormous garage or parking lot, which had long been needed. And to cap such conversations there was always someone prepared to bet that, in spite of conflicting opinions, it was useless discussing La Scala, for whatever happened in the future "the Milanese would rebuild it exactly as it was and where it had been, without compromising its virtues or, needless to say, correcting its defects."

There were similar arguments among his friends and colleagues at work but he seldom got involved in them. He listened, but in a rather detached fashion, seeing little point in empty discussion. Nor was he in any hurry to go and see the bombed Scala.

Three days later, quite by chance, he found himself in front of the opera house. That morning a gang of workmen in the piazza were piling up what remained of the huge beams that for more than a century and a half had supported the ceiling—large lengths of squared timber, charred in places but still showing, in the parts untouched by fire, the clear pattern of graining. Wandering inside the building, he found that the most disturbing and unnatural feature was not so much the crunch of rubble underfoot as the daylight streaming through the jagged hole in the roof. Although it was a calm, bright morning, the light seemed unbelievably cold, as if engendered by the very ruins it illuminated or by the building itself, which had never been penetrated by natural daylight. It was more than cold; it was impure.

He realized in a flash that some kind of holiness had been violated, that the affront was not just to this particular theatre, renowned as it was, but to all similar places, large and small. And as he stood there he was overcome by nostalgia. Memories came flooding back, swirling about in no semblance of shape or sequence, some of them significant, others trivial. Confused though these recollections were, they helped to clear his mind. This destruction, this silence filled only with the ghosts of memory, verified what he had so often thought and felt during the war years, especially when the outlook was at its bleakest, with no certainty of any future. The only enduring thing was art, and the only true people were the characters created by artistic imagination. They remained true and constant, unaffected by circumstances, and in times of hardship they alone gave meaning to life and guarantee of a future.

That promise made it certain that La Scala would rise once more; its task was not finished.

La Scala did, in fact, live again. On the night of 11 May 1946 Toscanini mounted the rostrum of the restored theatre to conduct a concert of Italian music. His presence alone made it much more than an evening of exceptional musical delight, and the significance of the occasion was not lost on the audience. It was not just that the war was over or that the poignant words of the chorus from *Nabucco* were so allusive. This was the beginning of a new era. The three thousand people in the audience may not have been aware that the white of the reconstructed auditorium had lost the golden overtones acquired over years of seasoning, so that it now had a milky appearance, but no matter. They were here to see La Scala reborn.

Raul Radice

LA SCALA
FROM 1946 UNTIL TODAY

On the evening of 11 May 1946 Milan's opera house reopened. The great theatre had been rebuilt along the old lines, the scars of war healed with such loving care as to be quite imperceptible. Older members of the audience greeted one another emotionally; and there on the rostrum, returning after long years of exile, was the Maestro himself, the incomparable Toscanini. In an unbelievably short time, taking priority over many other public buildings which still required years of work for full restoration, La Scala had emerged from the ruins, ready to assume its rightful place as the focal point of the city's social and cultural life.

Those who were privileged to be present on this occasion and to hear Toscanini conduct the first postwar concert sensed that great things were again in store. La Scala looked more splendid than ever. From outside little seemed changed but in fact there had been important structural improvements. Luigi Lorenzo Secchi, the architect, had repaired the damaged exterior and faithfully restored the interior decorations in accordance with the original plans of Piermarini and Sanquirico. The old ceiling and its magnificent chandelier were meticulously reproduced, but in fact the entire roof had been reconstructed in steel, and any worries that this might have an adverse effect on the hall's acoustics were soon allayed. Secchi had also taken the opportunity to modernize other features of the house in readiness for the new opera season, which was due to begin on the evening of December 26.

Prior to the official reopening, La Scala had given a summer season of opera, from July 27 until September 29, at the Palazzo dello Sport. The repertory comprised *Mefistofele, Tosca, Le Tricorne, Aïda, Rigoletto, Lohengrin, Carmen, Cavalleria Rusticana,* and *La Forza del Destino.* This had been followed by a series of autumn concerts inaugurated by Alfredo Casella. Now the company was back home, and the first postwar season opened with a performance of *Nabucco,* conducted by Tullio Serafin, produced by Alessandro Sanine, with sets and costumes by Guido Marussig. The singers were Gino Bechi, Mario Binci, Cesare Siepi, Maria Pedrini, Fedora Barbieri, Maria Teresa Bertasi, Carlo Forti, and Luigi Nardi.

The range of the postwar Scala's repertory was astonishing. *Nabucco* was followed by Rossini's *La Cenerentola,* Pizzetti's *L'Oro, Der Rosenkavalier, Samson et Dalila, Lucia di Lammermoor, Andrea Chénier, L'Amico Fritz, Hansel and Gretel, La Traviata, Don Carlos,* Massenet's *Manon, Tristan und Isolde, Rigoletto, Madama Butterfly, Orfeo ed Euridice, La Bohème, Die Meistersinger von Nürnberg, Così fan Tutte,* and the first Italian productions of Britten's *Peter Grimes* and of Claudel and Honegger's *Jeanne d'Arc au Bûcher.* There were also a large number of ballets, including *Petrushka, Bolero,* Johann Strauss's *Caprices Viennoises,* Goffredo Petrassi's *La Follia di Orlando,* Pick-Mangiagalli's *Evocazioni,* De Falla's *Le Tricorne,* Delibes's *Coppélia,* and Weber's *Invitation to the Dance.* Contributing to these were many famous singers, producers, and designers, together, of course, with a highly distinguished list of conductors, including Toscanini, Serafin (also artistic director), De Sabata, Antonio Guarnieri, Ettore Panizza, Sergio Failoni, Bruno Bogo, Ildebrando Pizzetti, Fernando Previtali, Paul Sacher, and Jonel Perlea.

Supervising and coordinating this wealth of musical and artistic talent was the new director of La Scala, Antonio Ghiringhelli. Just as the governing body had chosen an architect who had done much more than merely restore the old Scala, they now appointed to the highest post a "nonmusician" (not for the first time) who for some twenty-five years had been closely involved with the theatre's fortunes, first as a committee member and later as a director. Ghiringhelli was an industrialist and he had been nominated by Mayor Greppi. It may have seemed to the casual, disinterested observer that when La Scala reopened all the preparatory work had already been done. In fact, Ghiringhelli's task, like that of Secchi and all others connected with the house, was only just beginning.

There were all manner of things to be solved behind the scenes—suitable accommodation for scenery and costume designers, adequate rehearsal rooms, new dressing rooms and public amenities, not to mention the decisions to be made on more basic problems such as new heating and air-conditioning systems, electrical installations, and the search for new work premises at Bovisa.

Ghiringhelli, general secretary Luigi Oldani, and the various artistic directors (first Serafin, later Mario Labroca, Gianandrea Gavazzeni, and Francesco Siciliani) all had to surmount short-term difficulties, some of which arose from the success of single performances. But each and every one of them knew that there would have been no point in merely struggling on from day to day without being constantly aware of the need to resolve the complexities relating to the biggest problem of all—the future of La Scala.

They were all convinced that their primary task was to stimulate and educate the public. But opinion was divided as to the feasibility of reestablishing the old-style "opera season" which had led to the foundation of the self-governing corporation as against a season more realistically geared to present-day economic difficulties. Clearly, whatever the decision, it would be essential to organize La Scala around a permanent body of artists and technicians, for only when some measure of stability had been attained would it be possible to make contact with a new generation of opera-goers.

The men responsible for directing the fortunes of the new Scala decided that the public should be provided with a broadly based repertory which included not only well-tested favourites but also neglected works of the past and experimental modern operas. They set about reviving the tradition of ballet with a reorganization of teaching and training systems. The slow, patient work began to build up a permanent staff of orchestral players, chorus members, and technicians capable of maintaining the high standards of the house. The whole administrative structure of the corporation was overhauled. Provision was made for new, up-to-date installations consistent with the size of the building. The idea was mooted for extending the opera season into the summer; and it was agreed that steps should be taken to document the theatre's activities and to commission new critical studies to be published for special commemorative occasions.

These plans were already afoot, or at least agreed upon, at the end of the 1946–47 season, and in due course they led logically to further developments. One such was the foundation of an advanced school for young singers who were to be known as "Cadets of La Scala" and who gave performances of operas by Pergolesi, Cherubini, Sacchini, and others in Italy and foreign cities, including, to name only two, Wiesbaden and Paris. Then, too, a school for male ballet dancers was established alongside the one for female dancers founded thirty-four years previously. In addition to these there was a new school of stage design, another for choral singing, and a third for children studying to be singers, which was later to offer university students courses in the history and appreciation of music. In due course important modifications were made to the main building, notably the enlargement and opening of new foyers on the ground floor, at the level of the boxes, and on the two gallery floors, which had not been provided with such facilities for the past century and a half.

All these projects were undertaken on the assumption that the opera house would attract an ever-increasing public, opening its doors both to the working class, which had felt itself excluded in the past, and to audiences of all ages, who, although perhaps inclined to think of opera as old-fashioned, were nevertheless impelled by nature and upbringing to wish La Scala well. Some would obviously confine themselves to the traditional repertory but others, it was hoped, would come with a more open mind to hear works by contemporary composers.

So it was that a new theatre, remarkable both in conception and design, came to be built. The Piccola Scala, an offshoot of the main house, was inaugurated at the beginning of the 1955–56 season with a production of *Il Matrimonio Segreto,* conducted by Nino Sanzogno and directed by Giorgio Strehler. Although its initial reception was cool, the Piccola Scala soon revealed itself particularly suitable for certain types of music, notably chamber operas (both old and new), chamber concerts, solo recitals, and experimental works not likely to appeal to a large audience or to one with conventional tastes.

There is no doubt that La Scala was largely responsible for the great improvement in the music-going public's knowledge and taste in those postwar years. The famous opera house had already pointed the way in the course of its first season by adopting a policy which, while staunchly maintaining its illustrious traditions, showed a willingness to embrace new ideas, welcome contemporary composers, and encourage promising singers and conductors, both from home and abroad. And indeed there was an extraordinary wealth of talent which La Scala was quick to recognize. The list of native and foreign composers whose works were performed (and La Scala had not in the past been exactly receptive to new operas) is impressive. It includes Prokofiev, Gian Francesco Malipiero, Britten, Ghedini, Poulenc, Petrassi, Schoenberg, Pizzetti, Hindemith, Dallapiccola, Shostakovich, Peragallo, Sutermeister, Menotti, Walton, Riccardo Malipiero, Chailly, Nino Rota, Virgilio Mortari, Jacopo Napoli, and Renzo Rossellini. Many of the world's leading conductors stood on the Scala rostrum. The audience bade farewell to Toscanini after he had conducted a Wagner concert in aid of the opera house's staff insurance fund. In his place they hailed De Sabata, who was to make an international reputation; and from abroad came Furtwängler, Karajan, Mitropoulos, Bernstein, Hermann Scherchen, Schippers, Böhm, Krauss, Cluytens, Knappertsbusch, Erich Kleiber, and Prêtre. Young up-and-coming Italian conductors included Carlo Maria Giulini, Gianandrea Gavazzeni, Guido Cantelli, Nino Sanzogno, Bruno Bartoletti, Bruno Maderna, and Claudio Abbado.

The same high standards were maintained by those responsible for the actual stage spectacle. This department was under the direction of Nicola Benois. Here the official policy was to reject eclecticism, no matter how tempting, in favour of unity of style. To this end a number of famous artists were invited to collaborate (most of whom had not ventured into the field of scenic design before), as well as directors who, although renowned in other spheres, had not tried their hand previously at opera.

The list of artists was particularly distinguished. Caspar Neher painted the scenery for *Peter Grimes,* Ludwig Sievert was commissioned for *Ariadne auf Naxos,* and Foujita Tsugji for *Madama Butterfly.* Later arrivals included Josef Svoboda and a host of experienced artists such as Benois himself, Gianni Ratto, Veniero Colasanti, Mario Vellani Marchi, and

Cipriano Efisio Oppo. The roster was swelled, too, by artists whose names were at that time less familiar to the public, such as Mario Sironi *(Tristan und Isolde),* Alberto Savinio *(Oedipus Rex* and *Tales of Hoffmann),* Felice Casorati *(Fidelio),* Salvatore Fiume *(Medea),* Lila de Nobili *(La Traviata* and *Aïda),* Léonor Fini *(Il Credulo),* Giorgio de Chirico *(The Legend of Joseph, Mefistofele,* and *Apollon Musagète),* Gregorio Sciltian *(Mavra),* Renato Guttuso *(La Figlia di Jorio),* Piero Zuffi *(Alceste, La Vestale,* and *Murder in the Cathedral),* Giulio Coltellacci *(Il Cordovano),* Franco Zeffirelli *(L'Italiana in Algeri* and *La Bohème),* and Pier Luigi Pizzi *(Il Trovatore* and *Aïda).*

The list of directors included Giorgio Strehler *(La Traviata, The Love for Three Oranges, Il Cordovano, L'Allegra Brigata,* and *Ariadne auf Naxos),* Guido Salvini *(L'Enfant et les Sortilèges),* Ettore Giannini *(The Abduction from the Seraglio),* Roberto Rossellini *(Jeanne d'Arc au Bûcher),* Alessandro Brissoni *(Gli Incatenati),* Tatiana Pavlova *(Boris Godunov* and *Eugen Onegin),* Franco Zeffirelli *(La Cenerentola, La Bohème, La Traviata,* and *Il Turco in Italia),* Luchino Visconti (who made his debut with *La Vestale* and subsequently directed *La Sonnambula, La Traviata, Anna Bolena,* and *Iphigénie en Tauride),* Eduardo de Filippo *(La Pietra del Paragone* and Paisiello's *Il Barbiere),* Luigi Squarzina *(Fedra, Falstaff,* and *Manon),* Giorgio de Lullo *(Il Trovatore* and *Aïda),* Virginio Puecher (Busoni's *Turandot* and *Ali Baba),* and Franco Enriquez *(Master Peter's Puppet Show, Aïda, Manon Lescaut, La Donna è Mobile, La Fida Ninfa, L'Amico Fritz, The Barber of Seville,* and *I Puritani).*

Mario Frigerio, Carlo Piccinato, Giulia Tess, Margherita Wallmann, and Giovacchino Forzano reappeared in 1950 for a new production of *La Bohème;* and among foreign directors at La Scala were Hans Zimmermann, Oscar Fritz Schub, Pierre Bertin, and Jean Vilar. Otto Erhardt directed the *Ring* cycle, conducted in its original version by Furtwängler, and Carl Ebert directed Igor Stravinsky's *The Rake's Progress,* which La Scala put on in preview before its production at the 1951 Venice Festival.

Famous conductors, directors, and designers—these are just a few of the distinguished people who helped La Scala regain its former prestige and mount a succession of memorable opera seasons. And needless to say, the list of great singers is too long to be mentioned here. As in former days there were famous rivalries which added excitement to particular occasions, notably those of Maria Callas and Renata Tebaldi, Mario del Monaco and Giuseppe Di Stefano. Of all the dancers appearing at La Scala, the outstanding name is that of Carla Fracci.

This vast and complex undertaking, dedicated to attaining the best possible results, was bound to have repercussions throughout the international world of music. After the first outside performances (a concert given by Toscanini in July 1946 at the Lucerne Festival, followed by a concert under De Sabata in Rome during the same year), the invitations from abroad for Scala concerts and operas were increasingly numerous, particularly from 1949 onward. Within the next twenty years or so, after a season at Covent Garden when De Sabata conducted *Otello* and *Falstaff* and Franco Capuana *L'Elisir d'Amore,* Karajan conducted *Don Giovanni* in Munich and *Lucia di Lammermoor* at the Berlin and Vienna festivals, together with Sanzogno in *Il Matrimonio Segreto.* At the Johannesburg Festival, Sanzogno conducted Cimarosa and Donizetti operas while Cantelli conducted *Così fan Tutte.* In 1957, at the eleventh Edinburgh Festival, La Scala gave *La Sonnambula* under Votto, *Il Matrimonio Segreto* and *L'Elisir d'Amore* under Sanzogno, and *Il Turco in Italia,* conducted by Gavazzeni. Both *Il Matrimonio Segreto* and *Tosca* were performed in Brussels. But perhaps the most important and eagerly awaited foreign tour was in September 1964, when the Scala company visited Moscow. The repertory consisted of *Turandot* and *Il*

Trovatore under Gavazzeni, *Lucia di Lammermoor* and *The Barber of Seville* under Sanzogno, and *La Bohème* and Verdi's *Requiem,* conducted by Karajan.

The Moscow tour was also a marvellous organizational effort on the part of all those associated with La Scala. The artistic merits of the Scala productions, often perpetuated on disk, went without saying; but this ambitious enterprise went to show that much progress had been made toward solving problems that had once seemed impossible. Yet the very success of the venture was to pose new, equally difficult problems for the corporation—the price, contradictory though it may seem, of any form of progress in any field.

Paolo Grassi, who had succeeded Ghiringhelli after twenty-six years of devoted service to the opera house, was well aware of the magnitude of his task. Ghiringhelli had loved La Scala obsessively, but he had preferred not to give too much publicity to many of the dramatic episodes that had occasionally ruffled the calm of his administration. Grassi, who was director for five years, was no less dedicated to La Scala but never hesitated to voice his opinions, outside the theatre if need be, at certain times of crisis. At one point he sent his letter of resignation to the mayor of Milan, but this was subsequently withdrawn after a unanimous press campaign in his support. This action eventually strengthened Grassi's hand, and although his term at La Scala was to be concluded a few months later when he was appointed president of Rai-Radiotelevisione Italiana, he was able to point proudly to the work that had been achieved under his directorship, "together with vice-president Belgiojoso, the artistic director Bogianckino, the present artistic adviser Francesco Siciliani, with Claudio Abbado, general secretary Nanni, director of productions Tito Varisco, chorus master Romano Gandolfi, stage manager Luigi Lorenzo Secchi, and many other highly gifted colleagues."

This work, unrecognized by the general public, was indeed impressive. It included the setting up of the archive and record office; the reorganization of the administrative services and the personnel and general business departments in new premises in Via Broletto and Via Ugo Foscolo (the latter municipal); the renewal of the agreement between the Comune and the opera house; the acquisition of a Honeywell computer; the installation of a closed-circuit television and radiophonic system linking the stage, the offices, the different departments, and the rehearsal rooms; an office working in conjunction with the trade union council CGIL-CISL-UIL, run by Silvestro Severgnini, which opened the doors of La Scala to a vast new audience of workers and young people; hundreds of performances in the provinces; a consistent campaign to promote modern music; an expansion of the publicity department and library, the preparation of new programs, close cooperation with the board for provincial tourism, and an agreement with the Electa publishing house; additional support for the singing and dancing schools with the aid of the educational authorities of the Lombardy region; and an enlargement of the book and record libraries of these schools.

Much was achieved, too, in the administrative sphere. This comprised financial arrangements with a view to balancing the budget; activities in conjunction with elementary and secondary schools in Milan and the provinces, and collaboration with these schools to enable students to enter the Piccola Scala; charitable work on behalf of the Associazione Amici del Loggione, designed to raise the musical and cultural standards of the gallery-goers; competitions and examinations for the posts of general secretary and director of personnel; four competitions for vacant places in the orchestra and another for admission to the chorus; the appointment, by means of an examination, of a new assistant to the head scene-changer, a new lighting engineer; the appointment of almost a whole new board of directors, following resignations and retirements; more publicity material in the theatre programs; the appointment of a new head of the box office; closer links with the cultural departments of the Comune and with the provincial tourist board; practical collaboration with the Piccola Scala, the Conservatory, and the Scala theatre museum; and an expansion of the opera house's recording activities.

The list of achievements was still not complete, for during that brief period there was much new construction work and technical improvement. It was typical of the punctilious Grassi that he should not even omit from his list the pulleys on the stage and the sanitation arrangements. Improvements to the house included new exits and emergency stairs, new rooms for the orchestra, a new telephone exchange, an overhaul of the air-conditioning system, a new elevator from the stage to the Via Verdi entrance, new dressing rooms for the dancers, a new curtain to replace the old one (after eighty years of service), new underground ticket offices, a new electronically operated lighting system, a new mechanism for raising the piano from the orchestra, and, finally, new electronic apparatus for the automatic changing of the movable stage sets.

All these improvements were designed to increase the efficiency of the theatre and to benefit both the opera audiences and all who worked in the opera house itself. They won the approval of local opera lovers and impressed visitors from abroad. During the period of Grassi's directorship, there were several well-publicized foreign tours. The second visit to Russia, ten years after the first, gave the company a chance to present five operas, *Simon Boccanegra, Aïda, Norma, La Cenerentola,* and *Tosca,* plus Verdi's *Requiem.* A visit to Covent Garden was reciprocated when the London company appeared simultaneously on the stage of La Scala. The Queen attended La Scala's performance of *La Cenerentola.* "This was the first time," wrote Grassi, "that two great theatres exchanged places, performing their operas at the same time on each other's stage." Finally, there was a visit to Washington for the bicentenary year of the United States. Right up to the last moment this was fraught with problems, but thanks to Grassi's tenacity and determination, all went smoothly in the end.

The Washington trip was a triumph for La Scala. After the first night, when *Macbeth* was staged, Paul Hume, critic of the *Washington Post,* wrote that the world-famous Italian company had put on a sumptuous spectacle which could hardly be bettered by any other opera house.

At home another major success had been achieved a few months earlier with the production, after some opposition, of a new opera by Luigi Nono, *Al Gran Sole Carico d'Amore.* Both these undertakings, so strikingly contrasted, were in the true Scala tradition.

Since 1 March 1977 the new director of La Scala has been Carlo Maria Badini. The administrative council of the corporation, presided over by Mayor Carlo Tognoli, appointed Innocenzo Monti vice-president and Claudio Abbado artistic director on May 5. Assisting the latter as artistic advisers are Francesco Siciliani and Giorgio Strehler. Since 1971 the chorus master has been Romano Gandolfi.

Raul Radice

MACBETH AT LA SCALA

A Reminiscence by Attilio Bertolucci

My friends in Milan were sorry that they hadn't been able to get me the ticket I so desperately wanted; and as the time grew nearer, the more I felt how bitter it would be if I missed it. Surely, having listened so many times to Leinsdorf's LP version, with Warren's inimitable shudder at the words "immobil terra," I deserved to see it on the stage of La Scala. Goethe had talked about "Shakespeare now and forever"; and in this case one was certainly justified in referring to "Verdi now and forever," for in this opera—even more miraculously than in Otello *or in* Falstaff— *Shakespeare and Verdi had blended in perfect unison.*

Every time I heard Banquo utter his agonized cry of "Accorrete, accorrete tutti . . . É morto assassinato il re Duncano!" I would get up in an almost drugged stupor, intoxicated in the sense that Beethoven must have meant when he wrote, in his letter to Bettina Brentano about the superiority of music both to philosophy and poetry, "Because music intoxicates like wine. . . ."

The last performance was to take place on January 9 and, just in time, one of my friends gave me a piece of advice: "Telephone the box office—I'll give you the number—and make sure to say that you're calling long-distance from Rome."

I lost no time in putting through the call, and a calm, confident woman's voice answered, probably a bit taken aback at my excitement. Lo and behold, it was settled. Two seats in the orchestra, previously quite unattainable, reserved exclusively for some mysterious clique of Milanese, and now booked in my name, definitely and irrevocably, provided someone could pick them up that afternoon. I made sure of that.

So, in the clear blue haze of that winter of 1976, the image of La Scala beckoned me, as if conjured up by magic, like some city of minarets and fountains in the Thousand and One Nights, *shimmering in the desert heat.*

We wished, as we set out on the long drive to Milan, that all our compatriots could have shared our happiness and sense of privilege. Here we were, getting nearer every moment to the city, that small capital of the land of opera which, in the words of the great Verdian Bruno Barilli, "invented true stories." We were lighthearted, absent-minded, in a kind of trance.

When we got there we felt like provincials. It was our first visit to La Scala, just as it had been for Stendhal, then an officer of the "young army crossing Europe," who, a mere apprentice of art and life, had entered that temple of music (not an inappropriate metaphor when applied to Piermarini's classical-romantic style of architecture) and found it an unforgettable experience.

We took our seats with the rest of the audience. People chatted to one another and waved to their friends; the orchestra tuned up. A few people were wearing evening dress but I was relieved that it was not an elegant occasion, if for no other reason than I have never learned how to do up a bow tie and a ready-made one is not quite the done thing. The fashions were indeed varied—as democratic an audience, I felt, as one was likely to meet anywhere. And the theatre itself was extremely beautiful. The typically eighteenth- and nineteenth-century gilding, which also adorns many smaller Italian opera houses, put me in mind of the gilded café signs described by Leopardi in Pisa during that carefree period when, "with renewed inspiration," after a long silence, he wrote A Silvia.

What distinguished La Scala from the other theatres was its size. This was obvious as my eyes roamed around the crowded auditorium while the lights were still up, but even more striking when the curtain was finally raised on the huge stage. Now, at last, we were immersed in the drama of Macbeth, *neglected for decades, thrilling to the clash of sword blades, marvelling at the complexities of mental derangement and naked ambition, pondering over the profundities of life and death, responding emotionally to the chorus singing so poignantly of their homeland ("Patria oppressa"), melody and words so sad yet full of hope.*

My expectations were fully realized. It was a complete and satisfying experience, in which I felt wholly involved, not worrying whether on some other night the performance might be better. As an opera spectator, I have the advantage of not being a professional.

At the end I rose to my feet with the rest of the audience, who applauded the singers with tremendous enthusiasm, no less excited than those people who were doubtless seeing Macbeth *for the second or third time. They clapped and clapped, and I had the impression that as they saluted the black singer Shirley Verrett, the younger members of the audience in particular were demonstrating their solidarity with all the world's oppressed nations. If so, I felt I had the right to stand beside them, for in my younger days I got the same sensation when listening to the voice—so proud and by turns wild and tender—of another great black singer, Bessie Smith.*

The hotel, not a stone's throw away, was comfortable, neither too hot nor too cold. Yet I didn't get a wink of sleep. I listened to N.'s regular breathing by my side and yielded willingly to the softness of the night, totally serene. For I had seen and heard a tragedy (not a melodrama, but a true tragedy by William Shakespeare and Giuseppe Verdi); and tragedy, purging the emotions through pity and horror, brings peace.

INTRODUCTION

by Paolo Grassi

In this modern world we are bombarded daily with photographs of all kinds—too many, one is sometimes inclined to think.

I try to keep an open mind on such matters, recognizing that there is much that I do not understand about photographic techniques and procedures. But it takes no great perception to realize that the hobby or profession, call it what you will, attracts many different types of people.

There are the hacks who regard photography merely as a livelihood, the amateurs who practice it for their own pleasure, and the true professionals for whom it is an art form, demanding total dedication.

Giorgio Lotti must certainly be ranked in this last category. I believe he is a poet of the camera. He has a poet's calm detachment, even when working in the most difficult circumstances, and the poet's unswerving determination to see to the heart of things and communicate his vision in a wholly individual manner. He has applied this poetic passion to his photographic interpretation of the extraordinary world of La Scala.

I have spent five years at this opera house. Like everything else, it is by no means perfect, but few would disagree that it is legendary, in the sense that it possesses a quality that is unmistakable, probably unique, different not only from other Italian theatres but from all opera houses elsewhere in the world. I marvelled at the way in which Signor Lotti managed to capture this indefinable atmosphere as he immersed himself totally in the daily life of La Scala, moving so quietly and unobtrusively, yet with absolute professional confidence, through the house—the auditorium, the stage, the wings—and becoming, for a while, one of us. I think that the results, artistically, have been exceptional.

It would have been a pity if such a splendid collection were to be left untouched in the files of a publishing house or if just a few photographs were to appear fleetingly in the pages of a magazine. So I did all I could to encourage someone to use a few hundred of the best colour and black-and-white photographs taken by Giorgio Lotti to make up a book on (if I may so term it) our Scala.

Happily, this was made possible thanks to the initiative of Editore Mondadori and the generosity of the Banca Commerciale Italiana. My old friend Raul Radice has contributed an excellent, affectionate text.

I think back on the five years I have spent at La Scala—happy and dedicated years—and feel proud to have conceived the idea for a book which is testimony to the unrivalled importance of a great institute of music and art. As La Scala celebrates its two-hundredth birthday, this volume of wonderful pictures will surely be welcomed by all opera lovers, both those who have come to regard La Scala as part of their lives and those abroad who may know it only by repute.

LA SCALA

La Scala under snow, on a typical Milan winter night. Many an opera season has been launched in weather like this, since for many years the first night of the new Scala season has been on December 7, feast day of Saint Ambrose, patron saint of the city. In the years prior to the Second World War, however, the house reopened on December 26, Saint Stephen's Day, so that the event was part of the Christmas festivities.

42

The ushers responsible for welcoming members of the audience and showing them to their seats are traditionally known as maschere. The two ushers shown here are in the "box of mirrors," a reminder of past splendour when the boxes were privately owned and each boxholder was entitled to decorate it according to personal taste. When the self-governing corporation of La Scala was formed, all the boxes were given a uniform appearance. But some of them, such as this particular box, were left in their original state for historical reasons.

Left: the carabiniere in full uniform who is stationed in the foyer on first nights.

The entrance foyer on an opening night. The first
night of the new Scala season, when times were
particularly good, was the pretext for an elaborate
display of feminine fashion. Audiences of more recent
years, however, have rejected such ostentatious
exhibitions in favour of more sedate and modest
attire.

Right: the foyer to the boxes during an intermission.
The bust of Arturo Toscanini by the sculptor Adolf
Wildt can be seen in the picture.

Students of the theater's ballet school put on a display and give out flowers for charity.

La Scala's chandelier as seen from the stalls, looking up (below), and from the top gallery (opposite). This chandelier, which has undergone quite a few alterations over the years, partly due to changes in the method of lighting, is regarded by the faithful as more than a mere object, indeed almost a living personage. At one time the chandelier was also renowned for the rays reflected from its crystals, which were carefully cleaned at intervals, the huge lamp being lowered from the ceiling by winches. Nowadays the crystal cups have been replaced by synthetic ones, lighter in weight but equally transparent. There are 352 of them clustered among the branches of the beautifully designed chandelier.

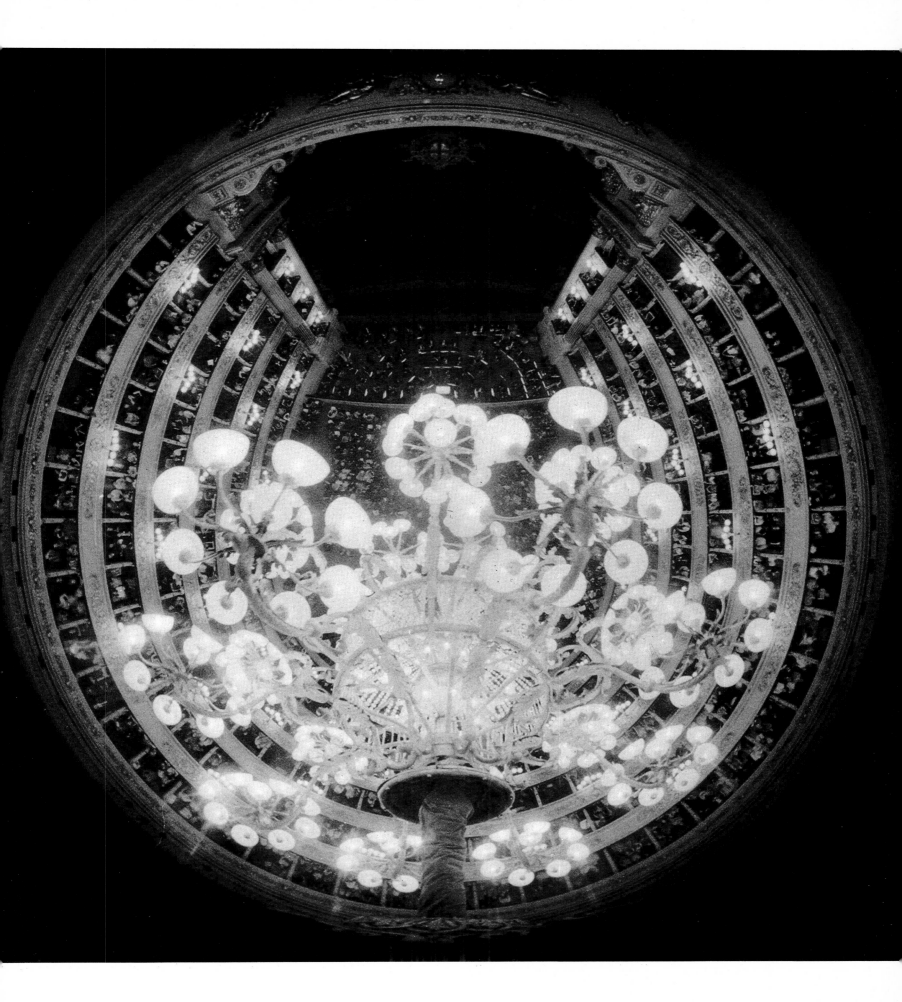

The theatre comes alive on performance nights when all the seats, at every level, are filled. The large central box (opposite) is reserved for important personages on official occasions, but is normally available to members of the public. The theatre has four tiers of boxes around the stalls and two galleries above. During a performance the atmosphere, even outside in the corridors, is electric.

BACKSTAGE

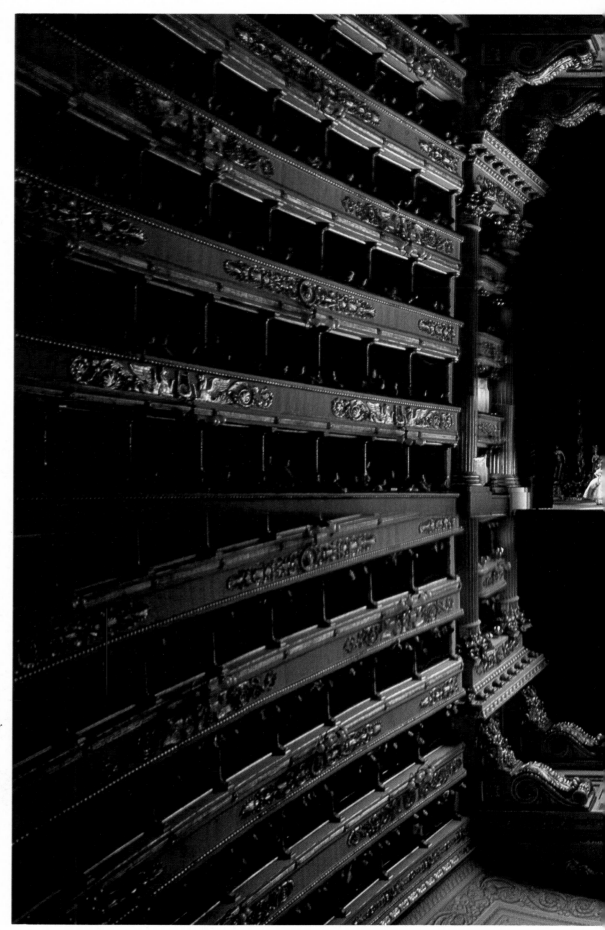

The miracles of La Scala

The photographer is always on the alert for an original picture, often getting an idea from the most improbable and unexpected circumstance. A woman engaged in the simple, everyday act of looking in the mirror of her powder compact was the inspiration for this double shot of La Scala, seemingly reflected upside down in the waters of an imaginary lake.

Behind the scenes

Most of the people involved in the preparations and successful outcome of a Scala production are anonymous as far as the public is concerned. At best, they may be known by name, but never seen. But without their hard work and professional skills no opera could even be staged. All of them play their part, as, for example, the shoemaker responsible for providing shoes, boots, and other assorted forms of footwear both for the principals and the members of the chorus. Equally important are the selection and making of the wigs, which not only have to be absolutely authentic for period but also suitable for individual performers.

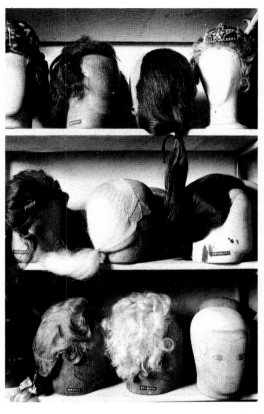

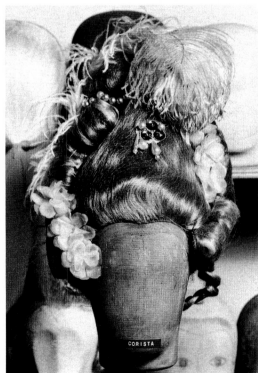

Hat making is another important behind-the-scenes activity. Hats have to be made to measure for particular operas, usually based on costume artists' designs, always bearing in mind the physiques of the singers for whom they are intended. Similar work is done by the theatre tailor's shop, responsible for all costumes and accessories. La Scala's wardrobe is enormous. In the Bovisa storerooms there are some ten thousand costumes, all easily available and in perfect condition, as well as accompanying ornaments and accessories.

Very often the sketches submitted by the costume designer reflect an ideal conception of the stage spectacle, and those responsible for carrying out the work have to use their ingenuity in finding materials that are not always commercially available. This is particularly applicable to coloured fabrics when special dyes are needed. Such an instance occurred with a production of L'Italiana in Algeri, *the sets and costumes for which were designed by Jean-Pierre Ponnelle (opposite), shown here with one of his own sketches.*

Flags, banners, icons, and the like are painted as required in the workshops adjoining the theatre's property storeroom. Here too are suits of armour, helmets, swords, and other weapons needed for particular productions. Furthermore, La Scala's stock of ropes and cables is perhaps unequalled anywhere. These are the kind used by every major theatre for scene shifting and for operating a movable stage. Ropes have to come in all lengths and thicknesses and most of them are made by hand.

The ticket office is open to the public every day from
10:30 in the morning until 1:00 P.M. and from 3:30
till 5:30 in the afternoon. All seats are bookable
after the announcement of the program. On nights of
performances when the house is not sold out, a ticket
window is kept open from 5:30 until the first
intermission of the opera.
The music archives of La Scala are important not
only for the day-to-day activities of the theatre but
also for research and spur-of-the-moment checking.
More than twelve hundred scores are kept here.

La Scala's theatre museum was founded in 1913, thanks to Duke Uberto Visconti, who was its first president. The first board of directors included Ludovico Pagliaghi, Ulderico Tononi, Arrigo Boito, Ettore Modigliani, Fausto Vimercati, Giuseppe Grandi, and Guido Cagnola. Organized by the Ricordi publishing house, which is an integral part of La Scala, the museum has on display items of considerable beauty and others of priceless value, such as the original manuscript score of Giuseppe Verdi's Requiem.

The theatre museum has been enriched in recent years by an extraordinary bequest — the library of 24,000 books belonging to Renato Simoni, donated in memory of his mother. The present director of the museum is Giampiero Tintori, shown here in one of the public galleries.

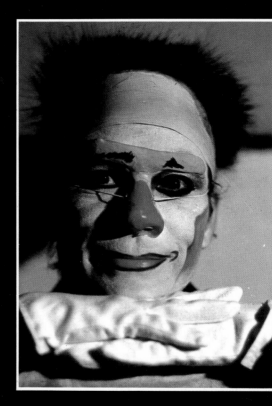

The art of illusion, nowadays opposed or rejected by the legitimate theatre concerned to show life as it really is, is essential in the world of opera, which almost always strives for this very effect. It is an art which is best judged from a distance, for it is designed for the spectator seated in the stalls and boxes. The farther away one is, the more amazing it seems. So the skill of the illusionist depends on being able to assess the precise effect his work will have on the audience. An opera house has to employ a whole team of people trained in this craft of make-believe. One such skill is the artificial ageing technique, which usually requires an hour and a half's work, sometimes much more.

On the left is the mechanism used for raising the stage for the chorus in symphony concerts.
Opposite: four separate shots of stagehands at work on an opera production. In the left-hand photograph the platform of the Castel Sant'Angelo for the final act of Tosca, with sets by Nicola Benois, is being moved into position.
The two photographs on the right show scene shifters handling parts of a building for one of the sets in Aïda, designed by Pier Luigi Pizzi (above), and another stagehand pushing a prop for the ballet The Nutcracker (below). In the bottom picture a wall is set in place for a scene in Carmen.

For almost twenty years Luigi Regazzi has been in charge of set building on the stage of La Scala. Regazzi, originally from Venice, is highly experienced, having worked previously at the Florence Maggio Musicale, Turin's Teatro Gobetti, and the Fenice in Venice. He supervises a team of fifty-six people, subdivided, according to the needs of a particular production, into small groups. Changing the sets between acts will normally take no more than twenty-five minutes. The heaviest scenery ever handled by Regazzi and his staff came from Vienna. It was for a production of Die Meistersinger and was made mainly of steel and canvas.

Vannio Vanni, lighting director (below).
Right: In the room above the chandelier the so-called
light followers (light engineers) operate the spotlights
that pick out the principals and follow their stage
movements. Below: two technicians up in the
heights.

67

All information and pictorial materials relating to the activities of the opera house are the responsibility of the publications department, directed by Carlo Mezzadri, and of the photographic service, which has been headed for almost thirty years by Erio Piccagliani. Contributing to the work of these departments, as well as to specialized publications, periodicals, and information pamphlets, are theatre personalities from all over the world, together with many foreign organizations whose activities all have to be carefully documented.

La Scala has received wide-scale publicity in another form since the 1976–77 season. On the night of 7 December 1976 Rai-Radiotelevisione Italiana was allowed into the theatre for the first time, relaying throughout Europe in colour the Scala presentation

of Otello, *conducted by Carlos Kleiber and directed by Franco Zeffirelli. The singers included Placido Domingo, Mirella Freni, and Piero Cappuccilli. During the intermissions viewers saw shots of the audience and of the stagehands at work. The producer Filippo Crivelli and the writer Giorgio Soavi also took part in a television interview (below).*

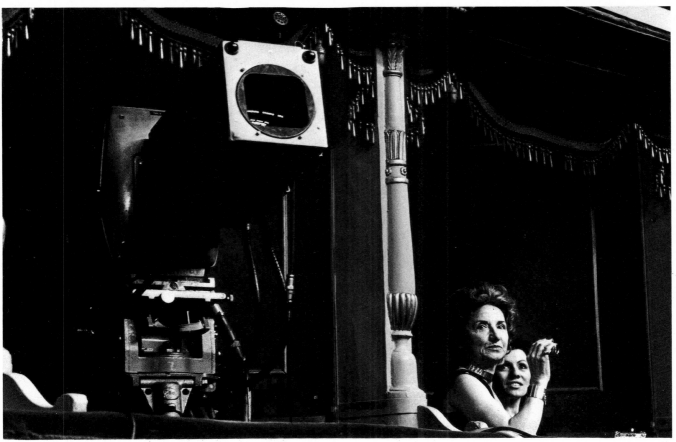

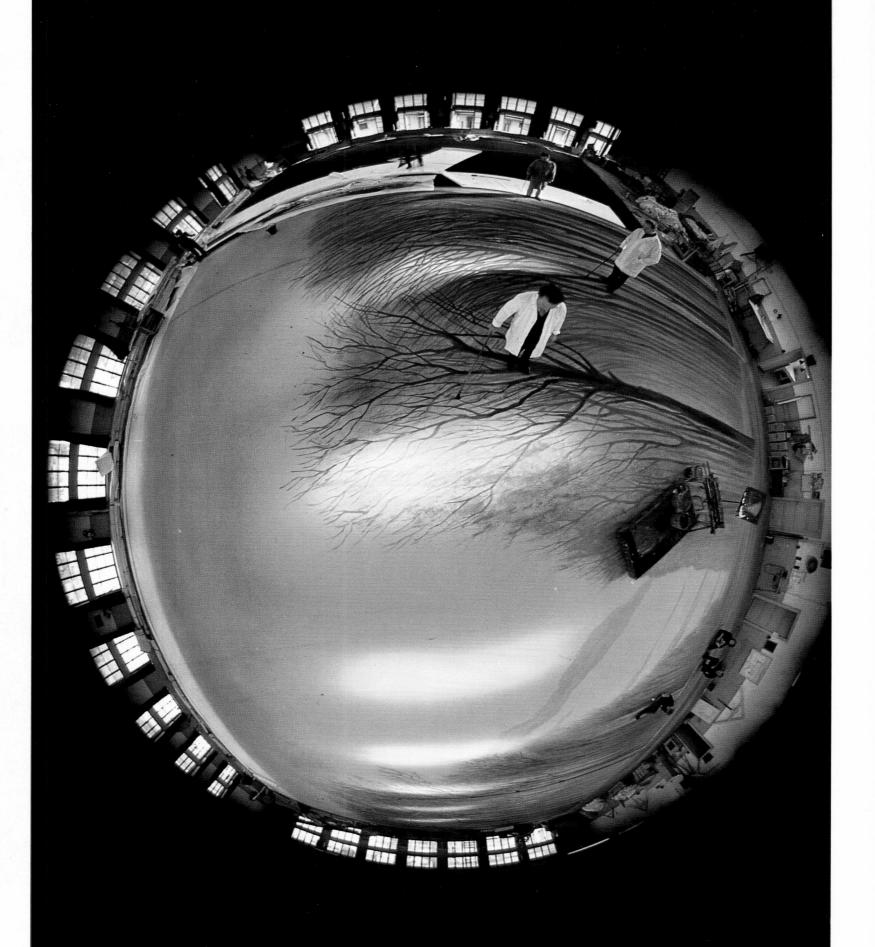

In the Bovisa workshop work begins on painting scenery for the ballet Swan Lake. The scene is to be painted on a cloth measuring some 60 square feet, laid out on the floor. Supervising the work is production director Tito Varisco. As a rule, there are three teams directed by three principal scene painters, each of whom has two collaborators and one assistant (opposite). The Bovisa serves, too, as a storeroom, some 50 feet high, accommodating many of the pieces of scenery used in previous productions (above).

The two photographs on the right show Tito Varisco and his staff working on the scenery for L'Italiana in Algeri.

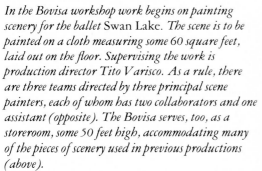

In the field of opera, as in the theatre, the role of the director is all-important. Not only does he imprint his individual style on the production but he also has to make sure that his ideas come across onstage. Thus theory and execution must go hand in hand, so that a good director needs practical ability as well as creative flair. Sonia Frisell, shown below alongside the bass Nesterenko in his role of Faust, has been one of the theatre's resident directors since 1974 and is the first woman to occupy such a post. Born in England in 1937, of Swedish-Canadian parentage, Sonia Frisell came to La Scala as an assistant director in 1964. The illustrations show a rehearsal in progress of the ballet Excelsior (center), the director's annotated score, and a scene from a production of La Cenerentola.

Francesco Siciliani, artistic adviser to La Scala, was formerly its artistic director (right). His name is associated with a number of Florence's Maggio Musicale productions, where he was director before being chosen to organize the music programs of Rai. Below: a press conference with the present Scala director, Carlo Maria Badini.

The press conference given by Ekaterina Furtzeva, Soviet minister for culture, during the first visit of Moscow's Bolshoi Theatre to the Scala in October–November 1973. Among those taking part in the conference, seen here, were Antonio Ghiringhelli, Minister Signorello, Mayor Aniasi, Scala director Paolo Grassi, and Senators Luigi Venanzi and Aldo Bassetti.

Paolo Grassi, during his term of office as director of the opera house, with Renata Tebaldi, Luigi Oldani, and Massimo Bogianckino. Oldani was then general secretary of the theatre and Bogianckino artistic director.

The new director, Carlo Maria Badini, between artistic director Claudio Abbado and general secretary Fioravante Nanni. Badini took over the directorship of La Scala after working at the Teatro Comunale in Bologna.

The Scala chorus is justly famed, its reputation passing on from generation to generation. It is notable not only for the high excellence of its singing but also for outstanding dramatic ability, conveyed on stage by a remarkable flexibility of mimicry and expression. Among many famous chorus masters at La Scala, Vittore Veneziani, who held the post during the period when Arturo Toscanini was in charge of the opera house's musical activities, was extremely popular. The present chorus master is Romano Gandolfi (opposite).

Much has been written about the important part played by the prompter, who has to work in close conjunction both with the conductor and the chorus master. Although never seen by the audience, any more than the chorus master himself, his alertness and sensibility are vital factors in the smooth running of the operatic performance. *Above: first assistant prompter Dante Mazzola. Above left: master prompter Stelio Maroli. Left and opposite: master prompter Cesare Alfieri.*

Maestro Claudio Abbado on the rostrum of La Scala. Formerly permanent conductor of the orchestra, Abbado is now the theatre's artistic director. Descended from a family of musicians, Abbado came to La Scala as a very young man, having already made a reputation at home and abroad, conducting foreign orchestras. He took on a post at the opera house after exhaustive studies and a testing apprenticeship in the fields of symphonic and chamber music. Especially noteworthy have been his critical revisions of some of Rossini's operas – The Barber of Seville, La Cenerentola, and L'Italiana in Algeri.

Close-ups of the Scala orchestra together with a panoramic view of the whole orchestra and chorus during a concert performance. The concert series regularly organized by the theatre are no less important than the opera seasons themselves. At one time the orchestral players were hired on a seasonal basis, but today the orchestra is a permanent body of musicians, comprising 158 men and 10 women. The photograph of the two players rehearsing under a portrait of Lenin was taken during a visit of La Scala to the Soviet Union. The harp is traditionally a woman's instrument and this is true, too, in the Scala orchestra.

Opposite: a few of the many distinguished conductors who have appeared on the podium of La Scala. Left: the Austrian conductor Karl Böhm, a fine interpreter of Beethoven and Mozart, who conducted Fidelio in the 1974–75 season and Così fan Tutte the following year. Above right: Gianandrea Gavazzeni, who was also artistic director for a time. He has been responsible for rediscovering a number of neglected operas, including Donizetti's Anna Bolena, which was directed by Luchino Visconti, with Maria Callas in the title role. Below: Carlos Kleiber, son of Erich Kleiber, who made his debut at La Scala during the 1975–76 season with Der Rosenkavalier and opened in the 1976–77 season with Otello.

Right: the Soviet cellist, composer, and conductor Mstislav Rostropovich, who appeared at La Scala both as soloist and conductor during the 1974 concert season (above). Francesco Molinari-Pradelli with the principal singers in Tosca, performed during a tour to the Soviet Union (below).

Opposite: The French conductor Georges Prêtre (above) has been warmly received on many occasions at La Scala. Among the operas he has conducted are Gounod's Faust, Puccini's La Bohème, Ravel's L'Heure Espagnole and L'Enfant et les Sortilèges, and Debussy's Pelléas et Mélisande. Below: the Trieste-born Edoardo Müller, who conducted Prokofiev's Love for Three Oranges at La Scala, here seen with the Soviet ballerina Maya Plisetskaya in the title role of Carmen Suite. This page: some glimpses of memorable occasions in La Scala's history. Below: Ashley Lawrence, musical director of London's Royal Ballet,

(below), after a performance of Schoenberg's Transfigured Night. With him are Vera Colombo and Roberto Fascilla.

Following pages: Claudio Abbado on the Scala podium conducting Verdi's Requiem.

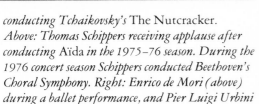

conducting Tchaikovsky's The Nutcracker. Above: Thomas Schippers receiving applause after conducting Aïda in the 1975–76 season. During the 1976 concert season Schippers conducted Beethoven's Choral Symphony. Right: Enrico de Mori (above) during a ballet performance, and Pier Luigi Urbini

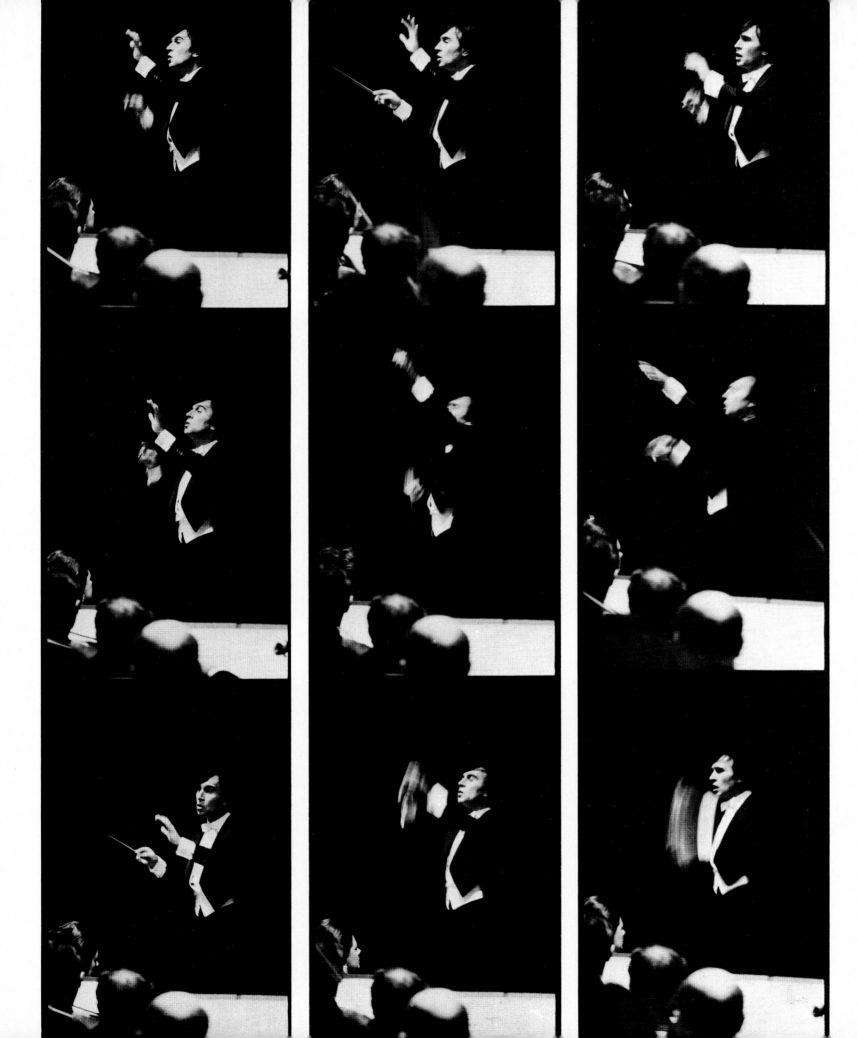

THE OPERA

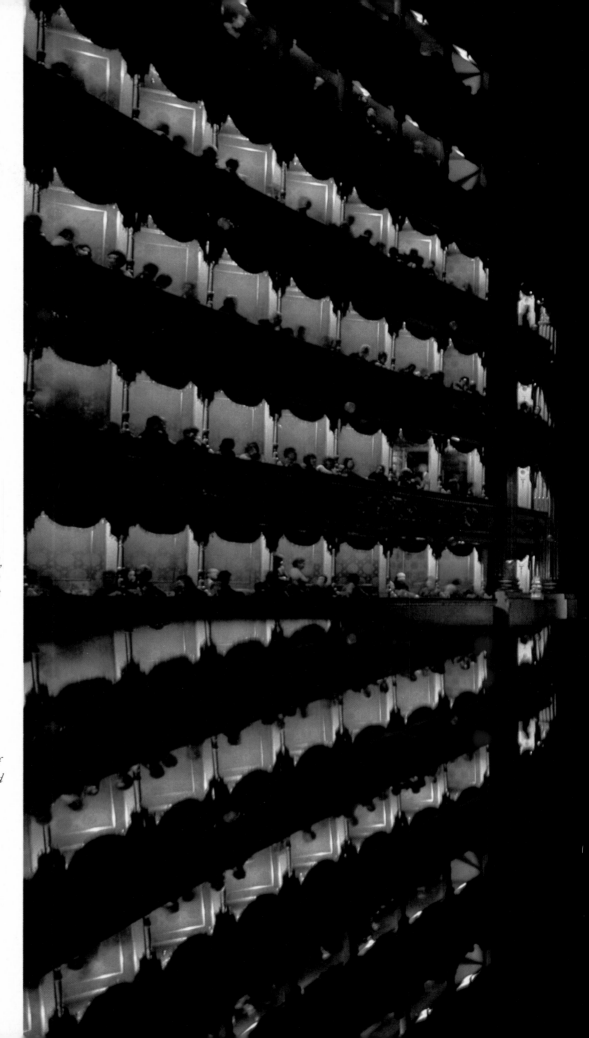

The supremacy of opera

No theatre can come into being without preconceived notions. Furthermore, because conditions and circumstances are forever changing, no theatre can remain narrowly, wholly faithful to the ideas and principles which inspired its foundation. Over the years modifications are inevitable, in keeping with changes in taste and custom determined by historical, social, and cultural developments within the country to which that theatre belongs. There is no doubt that when the Teatro alla Scala was founded, it was assumed that opera would be the predominant form of stage spectacle. Nevertheless, ballet and dance in general were not neglected, as evidenced by programs of the time. As matters turned out, the bias toward opera became increasingly pronounced year by year; and from the beginning of the present century until today circumstances have been particularly favourable for giving operatic productions pride of place. These are by far the most glittering spectacles offered by La Scala, and it is primarily as a result of the excellence of its operas that the theatre has gained international renown.

The policy of making critical revisions to the texts of Rossini operas was justified by the production of The Barber of Seville, *conducted by Claudio Abbado, directed and designed by Jean-Pierre Ponnelle; and Abbado followed the same procedure with* L'Italiana in Algeri. *For this opera, which opened the 1973–74 season, Abbado based his version on the revisions made by Azio Corghi for the Rossini Foundation of Pesaro, again collaborating with Ponnelle. Below and at bottom: a ballerina and Paolo Montarsolo, in the role of Mustafà. Right: in the foreground, Montarsolo, Angelo Romero, Margherita Guglielmi, and Laura Zannini.*

Another scene from Abbado's edited production of
L'Italiana in Algeri. *This Rossini opera was given
for the first time at La Scala on the night of 9
August 1815 and was such a popular success that it
was repeated no less than forty-nine times in the same
season. Since then the opera has been staged
frequently at La Scala, in 1823, 1828, 1836, 1839,*

*1846, 1933 (conducted by Ghione, with Margherita
Carosio in the title role), and 1953, conducted by
Carlo Maria Giulini. Abbado's version was
repeated in the following season. There is a strange
footnote to these facts. Another* Italiana in Algeri,
*composed by Luigi Mosca, with a libretto by Angelo
Anelli (the same one that was later used by Rossini),*

was performed at La Scala on 16 August 1808. Rossini's opera dates from 1813 and it was given for the first time that same year at San Benedetto in Venice.

Right: two more scenes from Ponnelle's production of the opera.

Teresa Berganza, in the title role of L'Italiana in Algeri *(left), receiving the applause of the audience together with Paolo Montarsolo and Laura Zannini. Below: a moment from the opera, watched by the stage staff. Opposite: the final scene from the opera, with the following principals lined up: Margherita Guglielmi, Paolo Montarsolo, Ugo Benelli, Teresa Berganza, Enzo Dara, Laura Zannini, and Angelo Romero.*

The 1971–72 season opened with Simon Boccanegra *by Verdi, conducted by Claudio Abbado and directed by Giorgio Strehler, with sets and costumes by Ezio Frigerio. In the title role was Piero Cappuccilli (seen here with Felice Schiavi, who sang the part of Paolo Albiani). Below left: Cappuccilli between Mirella Freni and Gianfranco Cecchele. Bottom: director Giorgio Strehler busy at rehearsal.*

99

Piero Cappuccilli (*seen below in his dressing room with his wife and a dressmaker*) *appears in the adjoining photograph with Mirella Freni. Another notable interpreter of the title role in* Simon Boccanegra *at La Scala was Carlo Galeffi, who sang in the 1933 production, which was conducted by Vittorio Gui. Cappuccilli, a highly accomplished singer of Verdi roles, has also appeared in other operas, including* Lucia di Lammermoor, Don Giovanni, I Puritani, La Gioconda, *and* The Marriage of Figaro. *Mirella Freni made her debut at La Scala as Nanetta in* Falstaff. *She subsequently sang Micaela in* Carmen, *Zerlina in* Don Giovanni, *Susanna in* The Marriage of Figaro, *Mimi in* La Bohème, *Violetta in* La Traviata, *and Desdemona in* Otello.

Opposite: Ruggiero Raimondi in the part of Fiesco (above) from Simon Boccanegra, *and Cappuccilli and Freni in an ensemble scene (below).*

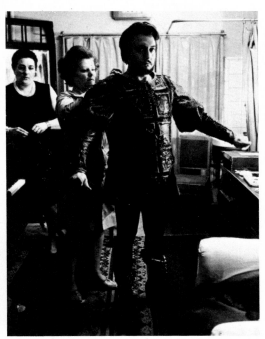

On December 7, opening night of the 1974–75 season, Fidelio *returned to the stage of La Scala, after many years' absence. The opera was directed by Günther Rennert, scenery and costumes by Rudolf Heinrich, conducted by Karl Böhm. The previous production of Beethoven's opera had been in 1960, when Herbert von Karajan conducted it, as Böhm did, in its original version. The revival of* Fidelio *and the appearance on the rostrum of the eighty-year-old Böhm had aroused some opposition and controversy, but La Scala's decision was well justified by the warm reception given.*

Opposite: two shots of the singer Walter Berry in the part of the governor Don Pizarro.
Right: James King as the imprisoned Florestan and Leonie Rysanek as his wife, Leonore. Below: an ensemble picture of the Fidelio *principals—Jeannette Pilou (Marzelline), John Macurdy (Rocco), Leonie Rysanek (Leonore), and James King (Florestan). In this production the* Leonore Overture No. 3 *was inserted between the first and second scenes of Act II.*

The Love for Three Oranges, *an opera in a prologue, four acts, and ten scenes, with text and music by Sergei Prokofiev, was one of the most exciting productions of the 1974 Scala season. On the left is an ensemble scene from the opera, below a quarrel between Truffaldino and the Cook, sung respectively by Sergio Tedesco and Giovanni Gusmeroli. Collaborating for this production were Claudio Abbado (conductor), Giorgio Strehler (director), Luciano Damiani (set and costume designer), Mario Pistoni (choreography), and Marise Flach (stage movement).*

107

Some of the many characters in Prokofiev's opera are seen here at important moments of the action. Above left: Luigi Roni with Rosa Laghezza, in the part of the Princess Clarissa. Left: Renato Cesari in the role of Pantalone. Right: another picture of Rosa Laghezza, attended by Eleanora Jankovic as Smeraldine.

The Love for Three Oranges *provided an opportunity for director Giorgio Strehler to exercise his creative and inventive talents to the full. Indeed, it is unlikely that he could have given them such free scope under any other circumstances. Prokofiev's inspiration came from Carlo Gozzi's comedy and the colourful world of farce and pathos portrayed by the author. To some extent, too, the composer was influenced by the interest displayed by Meyerhold.*

The great Russian theatrical producer regarded Gozzi's work as more than a simple tale about Truffaldino and Smeraldina, declaring that it signalled a revival of the theatre itself. Prokofiev went on to make contact with Diaghilev, the Ballets Russes, and Stravinsky, then travelled to the United States, where he wrote the opera. In the past Strehler had been noted for his self-effacing lucidity, but in this theatrical fantasy he felt justified in giving rein

to his imagination. This remarkable production was a conspicuously successful blend of old and new. Basically a free-ranging re-creation of the old commedia dell' arte, which had always fascinated Strehler, it reflected at the same time his awareness of the needs and aims of the modern theatre and his conception of future theatrical trends.

Richard Strauss's Salome *has been performed on numerous occasions at La Scala since its first production in the 1906–07 season. This was conducted by Arturo Toscanini, with Salomea Kruscenisca and Giuseppe Borgatti in the main singing roles, and according to the theatre records it had a stormy reception. From start to finish the opera aroused arguments and hostile comments. In the 1974 production of* Salome, *conducted by Zubin Mehta, the title role was sung by Gwyneth Jones, shown here with Siegmund Nimsgern in the part of Jokanaan.*

The most recent Scala Salome, *directed by Boleslaw Barlog, with scenery and costumes by Jürgen Rose, went back to original sources, based on a critical reinterpretation of a text stemming from the period of European decadence, one more suited to a freer climate of opinion. Opposite: the climactic meeting of Salome (Gwyneth Jones) and Jokanaan (Siegmund Nimsgern). Right: Gwyneth Jones in "The Dance of the Seven Veils." Below: Salome above the cistern where Jokanaan is held prisoner.*

Gaetano Donizetti's four-act opera La Favorita, with a text by Royer and Vaëz, has been performed some two hundred times in La Scala's long history. The 1974 production, directed by Margherita Wallmann (left), was conducted by Nino Verchi and sung by Piero Cappuccilli (in foreground below), Fiorenza Cossotto, and Luciano Pavarotti (the latter in the photograph at bottom left, with Bruna Baglioni).

Opposite: Piero Cappuccilli, in the role of the King of Castile, Alfonso XI, with Fiorenza Cossotto, singing the part of Leonora di Guzman. Below: Fiorenza Cossotto. Right: Ivo Vinco, as Baldassare, with Cappuccilli. This production of La Favorita, *with scenery and costumes by Tito Varisco, aroused some controversy, with clearly vociferated differences of taste between those in the boxes and the stalls.*

Produced in the previous season in the edited version of Alberto Zedda and conducted by Claudio Abbado, Rossini's La Cenerentola (directed by Jean-Pierre Pommelle, who also designed the scenery and costumes) was given again in 1974 under the baton of Pietro Wollny. In this new version the principal parts were sung by Lucia Valentini Terrani (left) as Cinderella, Paolo Montarsolo as Don Magnifico, seen opposite, above and right, with Margherita Guglielmi as Clorinda and Laura Zannini as Thisbe. Opposite, below and left: Luigi Alva as Don Ramiro, with the chorus.

Opposite: Paolo Montarsolo and the chorus in a scene from La Cenerentola, in a photograph that also shows the orchestra. Below: Lucia Valentini Terrani in her dressing room with her husband. Above right: singers Ugo Benelli, Laura Zannini, Margherita Guglielmi, conductor Pietro Wollny, singers Lucia Valentini Terrani, Paolo Montarsolo, Enzo Dara, and Alfredo Giacomotti. Bottom right: Paolo Grassi (his back to us) with Laura Zannini, Paolo Montarsolo, Lucia Valentini Terrani, Margherita Guglielmi, and assistant director Sonia Frisell.

Die Walküre, *second opera of the Wagnerian* Ring *cycle, conducted by Wolfgang Sawallisch, aroused lively controversy, mainly as a result of Luca Ronconi's production, for which sets and costumes were designed by Pier Luigi Pizzi. Ronconi's ventures in the legitimate theatre had sometimes unjustly been described as "profane," and it was predictable that he would depart from traditional conceptions of the cycle and stamp it with his own individual quality, as he was later to do again in* Siegfried.
Left: Jon Andrew (Siegmund) and Marita Napier (Sieglinde), who also appear in the photograph opposite, above. Opposite, below: Ingrid Bjoner (Brünnhilde) with a group of Valkyries.

Opposite: Ruza Baldani (above and left) in the role of Fricka; the Valkyries (right); Donald McIntyre (below) as Wotan. Right: Luca Ronconi and Pier Luigi Pizzi during a rehearsal. Pizzi also appears in the center picture; alongside it is a scene between Siegmund and Sieglinde (Jon Andrew and Marita Napier). Below: Brünnhilde (Ingrid Bjoner), braving the wrath of Wotan (Donald McIntyre).

Aïda *was performed in Moscow during the 1974 tour, conducted by Claudio Abbado, with scenery and costumes by Pier Luigi Pizzi, and directed by Giorgio de Lullo. Opposite: Fiorenza Cossotto (Amneris), Gilda Cruz-Romo (Aïda), and Giampiero Mastromei (Amonasro). Below: Fiorenza Cossotto and members of the ballet. Right: Giampiero Mastromei and Gilda Cruz-Romo.*

Left: Claudio Abbado (center) with Luciana Savignano, Bruno Telloli, Fiorenza Cossotto, Carlo Cossutta, Giovanni Foiani, Luigi Roni, Gilda Cruz-Romo, and Giampiero Mastromei. Below: Gilda Cruz-Romo (left) and Giovanni Foiani (right) in their dressing rooms. Bottom: the chorus lined up behind prima ballerina Luciana Savignano. Opposite: an ensemble scene; and Luciana Savignano (right) in her dressing room with the dancer Bruno Telloli. Both are also seen in the photograph at bottom, acknowledging the applause of the audience, together with all the other participants in the opera.

132

"If Janáček had been French," wrote Massimo Mila, "he would today be as important and famous as Ravel." Jenufa, which Janáček composed at the turn of this century, brings together a number of diverse elements ranging from naturalism to symbolism. Although it made an immediate impression, it did not become well known. In the Scala Jenufa, *conducted by Jerzy Semkow and* directed by Sandro Sequi, with set design by Renzo Vespignani and costumes by Luisa Spinatelli, the singers were Bruna Baglioni, Ruggiero Orofino, Renato Cioni, Magda Olivero, Grace Melzia Bumbry, Carlo Meliciani, Nicola Zaccaria, Nella Verri, Rosemarie De Rive, Luciana Rezzadore, Silvana Zanolli, Jeda Valtriani, and Maria Grazia Allegri. The center photograph shows Grace Melzia Bumbry in the title role of Jenufa. In the two pictures on the left Bumbry is seen with Renato Cioni and Robleto Merolla. Below: another scene from Jenufa, which Janáček based on a story by Gabriela Preissová, conducted by Jerzy Semkow. Botton: a shot of the chorus, ably directed by Vittorio Rosetta.

A revival of The Marriage of Figaro, *conducted by Claudio Abbado. Opposite: a scene from the opera (above); Hermann Prey as Count Almaviva with Daniela Mazzuccato (below left); alongside is the director Otto Schenk, who was assisted by Gunther Schneider-Siemssen (scenery) and Leo Bei (costumes). Right: Stefania Malagù and Paolo Montarsolo, in the parts of Marcellina and Bartolo. Below: Stefania Malagù (Marcellina), Mirella Freni (Countess Rosina), Theresa Berganza (Cherubino), and Daniela Mazzuccato (Susanna)—a wonderful quartet.*

Opposite: two more scenes from Mozart's opera, the first in the Countess's apartment, the second with Susanna (Daniela Mazzuccato) and Cherubino (Teresa Berganza). Right: Three singers wait in the wings for their entry cues. Below: director Otto Schenk, Teresa Berganza, and Mirella Freni in the wings. Bottom right: Figaro (José van Dam) and Susanna (Daniela Mazzuccato).

Carmen *made a reappearance on the Scala stage, conducted by Georges Prêtre. The title role provided a magnificent opportunity for Fiorenza Cossotto, shown in the bottom photograph with Nicolai Gedda as Don José. Other parts were sung by José van Dam (Escamillo), Adriana Maliponte (Micaëla),* Luciana Santelli (Frasquita), Nicoletta Ciliento (Mercédes), Nino Carta, and Pier Francesco Poli. *Directing* Carmen *was Mauro Bolognini. Pier Luigi Samaritani designed the scenery and Chloe Obolenski the costumes. Choreography for the opera was by Antonio Gades.*

With Carmen, *the board of La Scala in conjunction with the trade union council, CGIL, CISL and UIL, initiated its performances for workers in the 1973-74 opera season. These productions were also performed for the general public.*

Below: Carmen falls dead, stabbed by Don José. Opposite, above: Fiorenza Cossotto and Nicolai Gedda in the first act of the opera. Below: Carmen on her way to the arena.

Puccini's Tosca, *performed during the 1974 Moscow visit and then given in Milan, was conducted by Francesco Molinari-Pradelli and directed by Piero Faggioni, with sets and costumes by Nicola Benois. Left: the inside of the Church of Sant' Andrea della Valle, where the first act of the opera takes place. Opposite, above: Mario Zanasi, in the part of Baron Scarpia, at the end of the first act. Below: a scene from the second act — Mario Zanasi with Raina Kabaivanska in the part of Floria Tosca.*

Left, top to bottom: three glimpses of preparations for Tosca. *Putting the finishing touches on Raina Kabaivanska's stage costume; director Faggioni in the prompter's box with Cesare Alfieri; Nicola Benois, who designed the scenery and costumes, with the conductor Francesco Molinari-Pradelli.* Below: Kabaivanska and Placido Domingo in the scene where Tosca comforts Cavaradossi. *Opposite: the end of the aria "Vissi d'arte," and, at the end of the second act, the killing of Scarpia (right).*

Above: Tosca's final plea. The other pictures show the scenes preceding the tragic conclusion of the last act: the duet "O dolci mani," Placido Domingo singing "E lucévan le stelle," the appearance of Tosca, and the soldiers shooting Cavaradossi.

A revival of La Bohème, *conducted by Georges Prêtre and directed by Franco Zeffirelli, who also designed the scenery and costumes, in the edited version of Karajan. Above: three of the opera's leading singers, Paolo Washington (Colline), José Carreras (Rodolfo), and Ileana Cotrubas (Mimi), shown with chorus master Romano Gandolfi and conductor Prêtre taking their curtain call. Below: Margherita Guglielmi, with Washington and Giorgio Giorgetti (Schaunard), singing "Musetta's Waltz Song." Opposite: the death of Mimi (above); Carreras, Guglielmi, and Cotrubas at the end of the third act (below left); Carreras and Cotrubas (below right).*

The 388th season of opera at La Scala opened on 7 December 1976 with Verdi's Otello. It was conducted by Carlos Kleiber and directed by Franco Zeffirelli (also the designer of the sets and costumes), and it featured Placido Domingo in the title role (seen opposite in the "Esultate," with which the first act of the opera commences). Below: This opening night was a memorable occasion for another reason, for the opera was also shown on television in colour. Viewers were taken behind the scenes during the intermissions, being shown the stage, the light booth, and the singers' dressing rooms, and they were also able to see the audience in the stalls, boxes, galleries, and foyers.

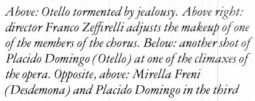

Above: Otello tormented by jealousy. Above right: director Franco Zeffirelli adjusts the makeup of one of the members of the chorus. Below: another shot of Placido Domingo (Otello) at one of the climaxes of the opera. Opposite, above: Mirella Freni (Desdemona) and Placido Domingo in the third act; below left: Desdemona repudiated by Otello. The small photograph shows, from left to right, Piero Cappuccilli (Iago); Franco Zeffirelli, Mirella Freni, Carlos Kleiber, and Placido Domingo acclaimed by the audience.

154

In Bellini's Norma, *conducted by Gianandrea Gavazzeni, the title role was sung by Montserrat Caballé, seen here above between Carlo Zardo, in the* part of Oroveso, and Ruggiero Orofino, as Pollione. *Opposite: Montserrat Caballé taking a curtain call.*

Norma *was relayed to television viewers by*
Eurovision. The opera was directed by Mauro
Bolognini, with sets by Mario Ceroli and costumes by
Gabriella Pescucci; and Bolognini explained the job
of a theatre director to his unseen audience. Below:
Paolo Grassi congratulates his leading lady. Right:
Caballé sings "Casta diva." Bottom: behind the
curtain at the end of the opera. Opposite, above:
Montserrat Caballé leads the chorus; below: two
scenes featuring Montserrat Caballé and Tatiana
Troyanos, in the role of Adalgisa.

Aron *had been performed for the first time at La Scala sixteen years previously, in Hermann Scherchen's edited version, by the Deutsche Oper of Berlin, and had been coolly received, with a certain amount of dissent, but this was not the case on the second occasion.*

Arnold Schoenberg's biblical opera Moses und
Aron *was performed in the original German version
given at the Vienna Opera. Conducted by Christoph
von Dohnanyi, it was directed by Götz Friedrich in
collaboration with Alfred Wopmann. Scenery and
costumes were designed by Rudolf Heinrich and the
choreography was by Erich Walter.* Moses und

The leading singers in Moses und Aron were Rolf Boysen, William Lewis, Gabriella Ravazzi, Maria Grazia Allegri, and Ruggiero Orofino. The first performance of the opera had been preceded by a serious fire onstage which would have entailed a postponement, had it not been for the dedication of the stage staff, who managed to repair the damage in record time. So the schedule was kept. The Scala audience, aware of the hard work that had been done and the risks taken, gave a special applause to the stagehands.

Gounod's Faust *was performed three times in as many years, in the now-classic version conducted by Georges Prêtre, directed by Jean-Louis Barrault. Sonia Frisell was the assistant director, Jacques Dupont was responsible for scenery and costumes, and Flemming Flindt supervised the choreography. The opera had an excellent cast of singers. Opposite: Evgheni Nesterenko Mefistofele) and Elena Zilio (Siebel). Right: Matteo Manuguerra (Faust) and Evgheni Nesterenko (above); Nesterenko and the chorus (below).*

Staged at La Scala in 1952 and again in 1971, Alban Berg's Wozzeck *was presented for the third time under the baton of Claudio Abbado. The principals were Guglielmo Sarabia and Gloria Lane. Scenery and costumes were designed by Gae Aulenti and the opera was directed by Luca Ronconi. Gae Aulenti, whose name appeared for the first time in the Scala program, had previously helped produce other operas, notably* Le Astuzie Femminili *by Cimarosa, in Naples, and* The Barber of Seville *at the Paris Odéon. Left: Gloria Lane in the role of Marie. Opposite, above and below: Guglielmo Sarabia as Wozzeck, alone and with the chorus. Right: Marie (Gloria Lane) and her child.*

Apart from the music itself, the particularly interesting feature of Debussy's Pelléas et Mélisande, *in the last version conducted by Georges Prêtre, was Jean-Pierre Ponnelle's production. In addition to directing the opera, he designed the sets (which in one scene featured an enormous rotating tree) and the costumes. Stress was placed in this* version *on the psychological implications of the plot, clarifying, where necessary, some of the points in Maeterlinck's play that were merely implied and not expressed. The team of singers for this production was a fine one, comprising Maria Ewing (Mélisande), seen in the two facing photographs, above, with Thomas Stewart (Golaud) and Jorma* Hynninen *(Pelléas), Ann Reynolds (Geneviève), and Evgheni Nesterenko (Arkel), all in the picture at the bottom. Below: The huge tree designed by Ponnelle and an opening in it representing the window from which Mélisande let down her long tresses.*

In addition to opera, La Scala regularly stages song and opera recitals. One such evening was given by Renata Tebaldi to celebrate her thirty years on the operatic stage, accompanied by Martin Katz. The occasion ended a long absence from La Scala. Her program included excerpts from Scarlatti, Paradisi, Gluck, Beethoven, Rossini, Bellini, Donizetti, Verdi, Mascagni, Puccini, and Zandonai, and provided ample proof of her ever-fresh singing and dramatic qualities. The auditorium was packed and the tremendous ovation was a mark not only of the audience's approval, but also of its regret for her too long absence. In the large photograph, the singer acknowledges the applause with an all-embracing gesture. Below: a view of hall during the concert. Bottom: Renata Tebaldi welcomed by Giulietta Simionato.

Above: Teresa Berganza, accompanied on the piano by Miguel Zanetti, during a recital which fully reflected this singer's stylish quality. Left: a recital by the tenor Luciano Pavarotti, seen here with Leone Magiera. Above: Viewers in the Galleria Vittorio Emanuele watch a televised performance of the Verdi Requiem. Opposite, above: a concert by the flautist Severino Gazzeloni. Below: Claudio Abbado and the pianist Maurizio Pollini in a concert given for workers from Sesto San Giovanni.

One of the operas presented at the Piccola Scala was Bruno Maderna's Satyricon, *a one-act work based on the fragmentary manuscript of Petronius, in an Italian rhymed version by Flavio Testi. Opposite: Participating in the first Italian production of this opera by the Venetian composer who died so young were Giulio Chazalettes (director) and Ulisse Santicchi (sets and costumes), both of whom are seen, below and left, with the singers. Above: an extra, and, on right, Gabriella Ravazzi as Scintilla. Right: Edith Martelli, who sang Fortunata; below, in foreground: Alvinio Misciano (Trimalchio).*

Above: two of the singers in Maderna's Satyricon.
*Opposite, above: The Piccola Scala also performed
Giuseppe Gazzaniga's* Il Convitato di Pietra, *the
sets and costumes for which were designed by Mino
Maccari. Gazzaniga's opera was performed in the
version edited by Guido Turchi. Below: a recital by
Graziella Sciutti, seen with Antonio Beltrami.*

The large photograph shows the Scala audience, which plays such an integral role in the success of any performance at the opera house. Quite apart from the individuals of which it is comprised, the audience has a corporate personality of its own. Below: Giulietta Simionato is recognized during an intermission.
Bottom: Renata Tebaldi with director Paolo Grassi.

THE BALLET

The revival of ballet

*One of the most urgent problems facing the postwar
policy-makers of La Scala was the encouragement of
ballet and the training of young dancers. The school
for female students was reorganized and a school for
male dancers founded, both giving instruction in
traditional classical dancing and also modern ballet.
As in opera, the aim was to strike a balance between
old and new, using the most gifted performers at
home and from abroad. The photograph shows
Carla Fracci and Rudolf Nureyev in* Giselle.

Adolphe Adam's Giselle, *based on the book by*
Théophile Gautier, revised by Enrico de Mori, has
never lost its appeal. Balletomanes invariably
exchange memories of the great interpreters of the
title role from the past, eagerly awaiting the
appearance of a talented newcomer to take her place
in the ranks of the famous. In the leading roles on
this occasion, Carla Fracci and Rudolf Nureyev
received a tremendous ovation.

180

*Another famous nineteenth-century ballet is
Tchaikovsky's* Swan Lake, *composed on the
invitation of the Imperial Opera in Moscow and
performed for the first time in 1877. Although it
was not immediately successful,* Swan Lake *was in
due course performed in theatres throughout the
world. The Scala production had sets by Enrico
d'Assia and costumes by Federico Forquet. The
conductor was Enrico de Mori, and one of the
leading ballerinas in the part of Odette-Odile was
Luciana Savignano (above). Opposite and right:
two more glimpses of the ballet during performance.*

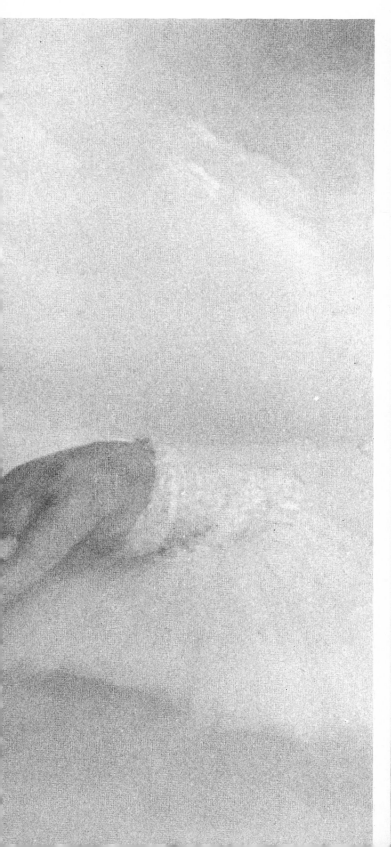

As the photograph below shows, the mists rising from the water and the muted colours help to establish the ballet's haunted atmosphere. Right: Carla Fracci, star of classical and contemporary ballet, in graceful action.

Three more shots from Swan Lake, *based on the choreography of Marius Petipa and Lev Ivanov, before the raising of the curtain and during performance. Left: Roberto Fascilla and Vera Colombo. Below left: Carla Fracci caught by the camera while limbering up onstage. Below: two dancers waiting for the performance to begin.*

Léo Delibes's three-act ballet Coppélia *was performed for the first time at the Paris Opéra in May 1870. The leading role was danced by the Italian ballerina Giuseppina Bozacchi, who died of smallpox during the Franco-Prussian War. In this Scala production the leading dancers were Vera Colombo and Roberto Fascilla (opposite). Right: Liliana Cosi, a delightful interpreter of the part of Swanilda.*

Above: an ensemble scene from the ballet Coppélia, *with Paolo Bortoluzzi and Liliana Cosi in the foreground. Right: Edoardo Colacrai in the part of Harlequin in Delibes's ballet. Costumes were designed by Nicola Benois. Opposite: another shot from* Coppélia, *with Liliana Cosi and Gabriele Tenneriello.*

"I saw the monument erected in Turin in honour of the wonderful tunnelling of Mont Cenis and I dreamed up the present ballet. It shows the titanic struggle of Progress against Reaction; and it is the greatness of Civilization which conquers, defeats, destroys, for the good of the people, the Spirit of Darkness which has held them in the shadows of bondage and shame." Thus did Luigi Manzotti describe the theme of Excelsior, a "choreographic, historical, allegorical, and fantastical action" in six parts and eleven scenes, set to music by Leopoldo Marenco. A scene from the Scala production of Excelsior is shown in the large illustration opposite. The other pictures show Paolo Bortoluzzi and Carla Fracci (left) and Aida Accolla (opposite, below), taking part in the revival of the ballet—an increasingly frequent event in recent years.

Productions of the ballet Excelsior, *following its initial success, have entailed quite a number of modifications to keep up to date with scientific discoveries and technological progress. Nevertheless, this has not impaired the effect of Manzotti's ingenious symbolism, culminating here in the final scene, which witnesses the triumph of Light and Civilization. Light is danced by Carla Fracci and Civilization by Elettra Morini.*

195

Shakespearean Trilogy, *the three parts of which are* The Tempest, Othello, *and* Romeo and Juliet, *was conceived for Carla Fracci by Beppe Menegatti. The first part, set to the music of Jean* Sibelius, *had choreography by Loris Gai. The second, with Antonín Dvořák's music, had John Butler as choreographer. The third part, based on Sergei Prokofiev's score for* Romeo and Juliet, *had* choreography by John Cranko and Roberto Fascilla. Sets and costumes were by Luisa Spinatelli. This page shows three moments from* Othello. *Above: James Urbain and Carla Fracci. Above right: James*

*Urbain and Amedeo Amodio. Right: Urbain and
Fracci.*

Two moments from Romeo and Juliet, *the one-act suite that Beppe Menegatti derived from Prokofiev's ballet. The one-act version was choreographed by Roberto Fascilla. Ballerinas who have danced Juliet in Prokofiev's full-length ballet have included Margot Fonteyn, Liane Daydé, Marcia Haydée, Vera Colombo, Liliana Cosi, and Elisabetta Tarabust, as well as Carla Fracci, who danced the one-act version with James Urbain.*

In The Tempest, *the first part of the* Trilogy, *many of the characters from Shakespeare's play make their appearance. Fracci danced Ariel, spirit of the air. Paolo Podini and Oriella Dorella, shown in the photograph opposite, were Ferdinand, son of the king of Naples, and Miranda, daughter of Prospero. Right: Gabriele Tenneriello and Amedeo Amodio in the roles of Stephano, the drunken butler, and Caliban, Prospero's savage deformed slave.*

The Dying Swan, *with choreography by Michel Fokine, has for a long time been one of the highlights in the classical repertory, a challenge for the great ballerinas. It is not surprising that this plastic poem set to the music of Saint-Saëns should give rise to an identification of the swan and its white wings with the ballerina herself, in white tutu. Thus the dying swan becomes the dying dancer—an interpretation* sustained by the great Anna Pavlova, considered *unrivalled in the part. The testing solo role continues to attract ballerinas of every generation. One dancer to triumph in the part is the superb Soviet ballerina Maya Plisetskaya, shown here below at the conclusion of the famous dance and, in the photograph opposite, performing the* Carmen Suite.

In the Scala's revival of Tchaikovsky's The Nutcracker, *Rudolf Nureyev assumed a triple role, appearing as dancer, director, and choreographer. In this sequence Nureyev is seen with Merle Park. The ballet was conceived by Nureyev as a vast dreamlike fresco.*

Three further moments from The Nutcracker, *which, together with* Swan Lake *and* Sleeping Beauty, *is recognized as one of the most important nineteenth-century classical ballets. Below: Rudolf Nureyev and Merle Park in Nureyev's own version of the ballet. Opposite, above: Nureyev (at the piano), again with Merle Park. Below: Nureyev, in foreground, with pupils from La Scala's ballet school. Sets and costumes for this production were by Nicholas Georgiadis.*

In Sergei Prokofiev's Cinderella, *conducted by Massimo Pradella, with sets and costumes by Germinal Casado, the Prince was danced by Paolo Bortoluzzi (seen in the large photograph at right, dressed in white), who also did the choreography. Below: Pierre Dobrievich, the ballet master. Bottom: Francesco Aldrovandi, making up for his part as the ugly sister Araminta.*

Three scenes from Cinderella. *Above: Paolo Bortoluzzi (Prince) and Luciana Savignano (Cinderella). Left: Bortoluzzi with Anna Razzi (Andalusian Woman). Right: Bortoluzzi and Savignano in one of the fifty dances making up the three acts of* Cinderella. *To create music that was powerfully expressive as well as suitable for forms of classical dances, Prokofiev provided a large number of waltzes, polkas, and mazurkas.*

The Scala ballet school in a photographic montage showing some of its activities. The school, founded in 1813, became what it is today because of the example set by many distinguished teachers, beginning with the great Maestro Cecchetti, and ballerinas who turned to teaching after their dancing careers were over. Pupils are admitted to the school at around the age of ten and remain there for eight years. Below: a group of second-grade students.

nal productions at the
ive exercise under the
va. Below: the director
al-year students.

Modern ballet

*Maurice Béjart, shown here at the back of the empty
theatre at the conclusion of a rehearsal in a trick shot
which somehow underlines the ambivalence that his
ballets often inspire, opened a Scala season devoted to
modern ballet from abroad. Béjart, now fifty, is in
charge of the* Ballet of the Twentieth Century,
established in Brussels in 1960.

"Ten dancers constitute the basic material and its multiple combinations. The eleventh dancer is stretched out and looks at his reflection in a mirror." This is how Béjart explained Karlheinz Stockhausen's Stimmung, a ballet for which he did the choreography. In the photograph at the top are the ten dancers, and at left the reflection of Stockhausen himself in the mirror intended for the eleventh dancer.

Nomos Alpha, *with music by Iannis Xenakis, the fifty-five-year-old composer born to Greek parents in Romania, was created by Maurice Béjart for Paolo Bortoluzzi, with the precise aim of contrasting "two instruments" (a cello and a dancer) and "two structures," one musical, the other choreographic. It was suggested by some that* Nomos Alpha *was the male counterpart of* Swan Lake. *Left: Béjart bathed in light. Right: Bortoluzzi in rehearsal.*

Apollon Musagète, *by now a classic ballet with
music by Igor Stravinsky and choreography by
George Balanchine, was originally commissioned by
Elizabeth Sprague Coolidge and first performed at
the Library of Congress in Washington for a festival
of contemporary music. It was conceived as an
abstract ballet, to be performed in tights. Below:
Rudolf Nureyev with Vera Colombo and Anna
Razzi. Right: Rudolf Nureyev (Apollo).*

The Miraculous Mandarin, *produced at La Scala with choreography by Mario Pistoni, sets and costumes by Eugenio Guglielminetti, was written by Béla Bartók in 1918–19 based on a scenario by Menyhért Lengyel. It has come to be regarded as an example of Orientalism as seen through European eyes. Bartók died, an exile in America, in 1945.*

Below: Mario Pistoni and Luciana Savignano. Opposite, left: the ballerina Savignano in her dressing room. Right: Angelo Moretto and Luciana Savignano in the ballet La Rivolta di Sisifo *by Aurelio M. Milloss, based on Goffredo Petrassi's Eighth Concerto for Orchestra.*

Left: *Luciana Savignano and Angelo Moretto,
leading dancers in Goffredo Petrassi's* Estri,
*performed, with sets and costumes by Corrado Cagli
and choreography by Aurelio M. Milloss, by the
Accademia Filarmonica Romana.* Estri *was given
for the first time at the Hopkins Center of
Dartmouth College, Hanover, New Hampshire.*

Above: *Amedeo Amodio and Luciana Savignano in*
L'Après-Midi d'un Faune, *performed with sets and
costumes by Giacomo Manzù and choreography by
Amedeo Amodio. The first choreographer and
dancer of Debussy's ballet was Nijinsky. It received
its premiere on 29 May 1912.*

In his choreographed version of Igor Stravinsky's Firebird, Béjart claimed to see in the composition the phoenix arising from its own ashes, "the immortal bird of life and joy, whose splendour and strength remain indestructible, imperishable." Stravinsky himself preferred the orchestral suite of Firebird to the staged ballet. Above: Paolo Podini in Firebird. Left: Jorge Donn (in center of picture) in the title role.

The theory that Mephistopheles represents another side of Faust, perhaps his double, has often been advanced. To some extent Gustaf Gründgens adopted this view when he arranged Goethe's poem as a ballet under the title Faust of Hamburg. A similar idea led Béjart to create Notre Faust, *to music by Johann Sebastian Bach, boldly linked with Argentinian tangos. Left: Béjart surrounded by Yann Le Gac, Judith Eger, and Quinny Sacks. Above: Bertrand Pie, Tom Crocker, Shonach Mirk (lying on ground), and Yann Le Gac.*

Three more high spots from Notre Faust, *with sets by Pierre Bosquet. Opposite: Maurice Béjart (masked) and Bertrand Pie. Left: Jorge Donn. Below: Shonach Mirk and Patrice Touron. Among the more spectacular scenes in* Notre Faust *are the Witches' Sabbath and the invocation of Helen of Troy.*

In Heliogabale, *created for the Yantra Ballet (Ballet of the Twentieth Century) and performed for the first time at the Shiraz Festival, Béjart drew inspiration from three sources — African music, used to conjure up the magical atmosphere surrounding Heliogabalus; Italian opera, reflecting the grandeur of Imperial Rome; and Verdi's* Macbeth, *expressing the power of the feminine will. Below: Patrice Touron and Shonach Mirk. Opposite, above: an unusual quartet — Michel Gascard, Shonach Mirk, Bertrand Pie, and Patrice Touron. Below: the full ballet with Pierre Clementi. Born in Syria of a priestly family, Heliogabalus was, from the age of five years, a priest in the temple of Baal.*

Béjart was spurred to create Heliogabale *after reading some pages of Antonin Artaud, whose poetic and historical writings dealt much with magical initiation.* "Ritual, love, and cruelty," *wrote Béjart,* "mingle in an exciting fresco, where East and West confront each other, where the sexes are confused and where religions meet." *Opposite: Yann Le Gac (in center of photograph) with Maguy Marin, Nyklas Ek, Tom Crocker, Michel Gascard, and Daniel Ambasch. Left: Bertrand Pie, Michel Gascard, Shonach Mirk, and Patrice Touron.*

The last performance of the Ballet of the Twentieth Century, directed by Maurice Béjart, was of Molière Imaginaire, *a comedy-ballet by Béjart himself, with music by Nino Rota and sets and costumes by Joëlle Roustan and Roger Bernard, and of* Per la Dolce Memoria di quel Giorno, *inspired by Petrarch's* Trionfi, *with music by Luciano Berio, choreography by Béjart, and sets and costumes by Roustan and Bernard. The latter ballet had previously been seen in the Boboli Gardens, Florence,* in 1974. In Molière Imaginaire, *Béjart was seemingly telling a story, availing himself of all possible means of theatrical expression, and at the same time echoing the sentiments of an artist pouring out his true bitterness. Opposite, left: Jorge Donn and Shonach Mirk in Berio's ballet. Center: the Ballet of the Twentieth Century, applauded at the end of* Per la Dolce Memoria di quel Giorno. *Right: Patrice Touron with Robert Hirsch, in the title role of* Molière Imaginaire.